WHAT'S NEXT?

BY THOSE WHO SHOW UP:
The *West Wing* Guide
to Progressive Action

SCOTT ROBINSON

ISBN 979-8345979167

Author photograph by Joshua Robinson

Remembering John Spencer

Also by Scott Robinson...

<u>What's Next?</u>
The West Wing Guide to American Democracy
The West Wing Guide to Global Politics
The Quotable West Wing:
        The Wit and Wisdom of the Bartlet White House
The West Wing Ultimate Superfan Trivia Challenge!
The West Wing Big Book of Superfan Fun!
By Those Who Show Up:
        The West Wing Guide to Progressive Action

<u>Red Brains, Blue Brains</u>
The Psychology of MAGA
Authoritarian We Will Go!
One Big Happy Family

<u>They Long to End Democracy</u>
The GOP
The Christian Nationalists
The Oligarchy
Minority Rule on the March (omnibus)

<u>Zero-Sum Freedom</u>
The Problem of Freedom
The Nature of Freedom
The Assault on Freedom
The Path to Freedom
The Future of Freedom
Freedom Confounded
Zero-Sum Freedom: Democracy vs. Oligarchy
        in the Battle for Liberty (omnibus)

Stand Against the Storm
How Democracy Feels When Autocracy Arrives
How and Why Autocracy is Threatening Our Democracy
What You Can Do to Defend Your Democracy
Embracing the Values and Commitments Democracy
        Asks of You

Three Great Forces Rule the World
Stupidity
Fear

Boldly Go!
Star Trek and Humanism:
        Living by the *Star Trek* Ethos
        in a Troubled World
To Summon the Future:
        Celebrating *Trek* and Human Social Progress
Resistance is NOT Futile!
        A *Trek* Handbook for Progressive Action
Chasing the *Enterprise*:
        Achieving *Star Trek*'s Vision
        of the Human Future
12 *Trek* Rules for Living

Pluribus: Joy & Dread in the Benevolent Machine

Table of Contents

"This is a country where women aren't allowed to drive a car. They're not allowed to be in the company of any man other than a close relative, they're required to adhere to a dress code that would make a Maryknull Nun look like Malibu Barbie."
Rights and Freedoms
143

"I'm the President of the United States, not the President of people who agree with me."
Working for the Greater Good
156

"I really like him, Leo. I want to hire him."
"What's the problem?"
"He's black."
*"So's the Attorney General and
the Chairman of the Joint Chiefs."*
Diversity
163

"We were no longer subjects of King George III, but rather a self-governing people."
The Essence of Democracy
170

"There are times when we're 50 states, and there are times when we're one country, and have national needs."
On the Other Side of Resistance
179

Bibliography / Recommended Reading
199

Introduction:
Those Who Show Up!

Democracy. It's messy, it's uncomfortable – but it's better than the alternatives, as Winston Churchill famously assured us. And it is certainly better than Authoritarianism.

The idea of a self-governing society, where all are considered equal, is humankind's dream. It's one of the things that makes *The West Wing* so attractive to its tens of millions of fans. The Bartlet Administration's vision for America is practically utopian – based on the conviction that the best government is one in which no one – *no one!* – gets left behind.

And especially now, as the opening decades of the 21st century have experienced an uncomfortable rise in Authoritarianism – not just in the United States, but in Europe and South America as well. It doesn't look promising.

This book suggests that we can look to *The West Wing*, not only for inspiration, but for conviction and a call to action.

The greatest challenge we're facing is that horrifying rise in Authoritarianism, as America has actually re-elected one. Such a thing is rare, thankfully, but not so rare that we don't know what to watch for. Even though we haven't experienced all that much of it at home, it has been part of the human story for millennia. We know what to look for.

This book is divided into two sections. The first – "Those

Who Show Up" –focuses on action we can all take to make our resistance real. Action that can push back against Authoritarian abuses and overreach. Action that can reset the scales, tipping them back in favor of democracy. Action inspired by courageous and compassionate moments from *The West Wing*.

The second section, "Know What We're For", reviews the principles and values that are essential to embrace in resisting Authoritarianism. These are *West Wing* values, liberal values one and all, to be sure; and they are also humanist values, which should come as no surprise. Put another way, this is a summary of *why* we answer the call to action.

The principles and values are based on some content published in three previous books, *Star Trek and Humanism*, *To Summon the Future*, and *Red Brains, Blue Brains: Authoritarian We Will Go!*, all by the author. The calls to action have several important sources:

- *On Tyranny: Twenty Lessons from the Twentieth Century*, by Timothy Snyder
- *The Bill of Obligations: The Ten Habits of Good Citizens*, by Richard Haass
- *"The Authoritarian Regime Survival Guide"*, by Martin Mycielski[1]

Each of these is well worth the reader's time, for deeper exploration of these ideas.

It's my hope that this book will both inform and inspire every reader, *West Wing* fan or otherwise, who is troubled by the direction the world is going and wants to do something about it. We've spent many years now, admiring the courage and determination and resolve of our *West Wing* heroes, with

---

[1] Found at https://verfassungsblog.de/the-authoritarian-regime-survival-guide

their firm principles and deep values. History is presenting us with the opportunity to follow in their steps!

STR
December 2024

By Those Who Show Up

BY THOSE WHO SHOW UP

The West Wing's Call to Action

Taking Action

Our *The West Wing* heroes are people of action. People who showed up to lead. People who showed up to fight.

When Toby Zeigler is confronted with the death of an unknown, faceless veteran he's never heard of, he moves heaven and earth to honor the man and his sacrifice. When CJ Cregg learns of monopolistic acquisitions among media corporations, she hounds her press gaggle relentlessly to get the word out. When Danny Concannon smells something fishy in the death of Abdul Shareef, he spends months flying to points far and wide, making endless phone calls, digging until he gets to the truth.

We admire their high ideals and solid core values – and we'll be discussing those, later in this book – but it's *action* that ultimately matters. It's action that defines leaders.

And it's action that we need now. Things are going in a bad direction, and how we each choose to respond will, to a large degree, define who we will be on the other side of it all.

Here's how our *West Wing* friends took action, when faced with their own challenges...

"I'm the God of Good Harvest in the Land of the Dead."

Break Down Social and Cultural Barriers

Will Sawyer, a globetrotting journalist who doesn't mind mud on his boots, is back in CJ's press room after a long absence.[2]

"Hey, are you a king?" CJ asks him. "Somebody said you were hanging out with some tribe, and they made you a king."

"I'm a god."

"Oh."

"I'm the only white man to ever witness the sacrificial rites of the Bau tribe of Fiji," he tells her. "I was almost a victim myself, until they made me The Supporter of the World."

"How'd you swing that?"

"Using my Palm Pilot, I convinced the Bau I had the power to make the gods' writing appear at will, and more significantly, predict the next day's weather."

"So you're a god?"

"I'm the god of Good Harvest in the Land of the Dead."

"I gotta go there and bring my laptop. It quacks when I

---

[2] In "War Crimes", S3/E5.

have e-mail."

"No, you're too tall," he warns her.

"What would happen?"

"They would paint your face and other body parts black so as to resemble a warrior ornamented for feast or combat. Then you would be garroted by a length of boar tripe."

"Yeah. No, good safety tip."

Donna is in Gaza with a diplomatic Congressional delegation, fact-finding for Josh and Toby. Colin, an Irish photojournalist, takes her on a behind-the-scenes tour, introducing her to locals who discuss their day-to-day lives.[3]

They visit a home in the Israeli settlement of Kfar Durom, where a mortar round had struck the kitchen two days earlier.

"It came through the roof," a woman tells her.

"One half hour later, my wife would have been giving breakfast to our two children," adds her husband.

"You must live in constant fear," Donna says with sympathy.

"You replace the tile roof with concrete and pray," replies the man.

"In Israel, there's talk of giving up these settlements," Donna comments.

"God wants us in this place," says the woman. "It is our divine, moral obligation to be here."

"If we give in to the Arabs, they'll take more and more, and eventually we'll all end up in Tel Aviv."

The Bartlet staffers hardly need lessons in diversity, but the

---

[3] In "Gaza", S5/E21.

point remains: we only *really* understand people whose life experiences are far removed from our own when we go out into the world and meet them face to face. When we spend time in communities far from our own, among people not at all like us, we almost always take on a broader perception of humanity – and this can't help but erode our prejudices.

"Travel is fatal to prejudice, bigotry, and narrow-mindedness," is how Mark Twain put it, "and many of our people need it sorely on those accounts. Broad, wholesome, charitable views of men and things cannot be acquired by vegetating in one little corner of the earth all one's lifetime."

Saint Augustine said it this way: "The world is a book, and those who do not travel read only one page."

And "He who never leaves his country is full of prejudices," per Carlo Goldoni.

And this particularly poignant observation from Marcel Proust: "The real voyage of discovery consists no in seeking new landscapes, but in having new eyes.

Using travel to faraway places as a means of pushing back prejudices and fortifying our defenses against the autocrat – who would have us forever divided.

Seeing the World

What happens when we get out into the world? What happens when we travel abroad, or even to the far corners of our own country? How do such travels diminish prejudice and bigotry, and expand our minds?

Travel is a powerful tool for dialing down prejudice and bigotry, exposing the traveler to differences in culture and worldview. It is by definition a willful departure from the echo chambers that we often live in at home, where we are surrounded by people who live much as we do and think much as we think.

Seeing how people live in countries and cultures other than

our own, or even people living differently in our own country, can be eye-opening in a number of ways:

- **Humanizing Others.** Prejudice and bigotry are emotional reactions to people beyond our social comfort zones that are stoked by those who would divide us – autocrats, oligarchs, religious zealots. The idea is to diminish our inborn empathy for those "Others" by dehumanizing them, characterizing them as less than we are. But when we step into their worlds and observe them, we see that they are much as we are, by no means "less", and as human as any of us. They become individuals, no longer stereotypes. They cease to be "Other", or are at the very least much less "Other", and empathy returns.

- **Expanding Historical Perspective.** When we experience another culture, we are often exposed to that culture's history, which will inevitably differ from our own. That history becomes a window into how that culture came to be, which bolsters our understanding of the people we're observing and meeting. It puts us on their level, as we understand ourselves by much the same process – where we came from. We may also get glimpses of challenges and injustices that helped shape their point of view, extending our understanding (and empathy) even further.

- **A Global Point of View.** The humanization and historical perspective from another cultural worldview mentioned above serve to instill us with a "global point of view" – an understanding, often elusive to those who live in the isolation of their own backyards, that our corner of the world is just that – a corner. And as we move out into the world, we have an increasing sense that it is, indeed, a world. This, too, extends our understanding of Others as much like us, further bolstering our empathy. People are, on many levels, the same all over, having the same needs, the same desires for happiness, love, family, security, and dignity.

- **Exposure to Different Lifestyles.** We are often convinced by those who would rule over us and divide us that the differences between us and those who live in other places make those people "strange", or that their lifestyles are "wrong" – that their daily practices and traditionss do not conform to the "proper" or "correct" way to live. When we see those practices and traditions for ourselves, and understand how they came to be, we move in the direction of understanding that there really is no "proper" or "correct" way to live, and that the differences are only that – differences. The people we observe are not "strange".

- **Exposure to Different Worldviews.** The autocrat, the oligarch and the religious zealot will all strive to convince us that other differences *are* "strange" and "wrong", even if we accept diversity in lifestyle: the values and beliefs of people in other lands may vary considerably from our own. Yet here, too, when we experience them first-hand and understand their origins, those differing values and beliefs come to make perfect sense – and we can see that they are deeply tied to the identities of those who hold them, as we are to ours.

- **Becoming the Other.** Travel to faraway places can be uncomfortable. Consider that when we are on foreign soil, or even in a far corner of our own country, *we* become the Other – we are the one who doesn't fit in. This forces us to come into confrontation with any prejudices and false assumptions we may be harboring, as those prejudices and assumptions surface in the course of new encounters. That may feel bumpy, but it is an opportunity for growth: we see how they take their own lives for granted, just as we do ours, and must grapple with the realization that our own prejudices and assumptions are actually grounded in ignorance – making us more open.

- **Challenging Narratives.** The false narratives that autocrats propagate to stir up prejudice and bigotry are often successful because they are absurdly simplistic; they seem to offer easily-digested cause-and-effect explanations that are emotionally satisfying (in the area of immigrants, in particular), and have no real factual basis. When we have those narratives challenged by our own first-hand experience, we cannot fail to see that the real world experience of other people in other cultures isn't simple at all; it's deeply and richly complex, and that complexity belies the autocrat's false narrative. We see that what we've been fold about who they are and how they live bears no resemblance at all to what we've been told.

- **Self-Confrontation.** All of these experiences, all this new information and observation that inevitably accrues when discovering new people in a new place can serve to inspire a process of personal reflection, in which a conscious acknowledgment that how we've seen the people and the place for a long time doesn't reflect who they really and how it really is. In this introspection, a kind of self-confrontation can occur: *What am I going to do with this new information? Should I change my point of view? What can I do with what I've learned, and how can it change the way I engage?* That self-confrontation can also cause us to closely examine our own sense of identity and privilege – *Given that I've been wrong about these people, am I really seeing myself and my own community as we really are, or do I need to make some adjustments there as well?*

- **Getting to Know Each Other.** And, finally, it's not just about our own observations; when we are somewhere else in the world, meeting new people who are part of a different culture, they are observing us as well. The exchanges that happen between us are as informative to them as they are to us, and it can be interesting and revealing to see how they are curious about the same things that make us curious – seeking to understand our values, our traditions, the things that matter to us. In addition to further stimulating our empathy, this can also expand our receptivity to diversity.

"We must find ways to bring people together across social and cultural divides," writes Robert Putnam in his excellent book, *Bowling Along: The Collapse and Revival of American Community.*

Beyond the Choir

Of course, we're preaching to the choir here. If you're reading this book, you've probably already done the work of excising your prejudices and bad assumptions, and embracing diversity. Diversity, after all, is a big part of what *The West Wing* is all about in the first place. It's likely one of the things that attracted you to it.

The point of this book, however – and the point of this section of the book, in particular – is identifying ways that Wingnuts can push back against the rise of Authoritarianism in the world today. And the point of this particular chapter is to suggest that, while it's a healthy thing for any of us to visit other countries and get to know people in other cultures, it's of particular value when the experience is undertaken by someone who *does* harbor prejudices, bigotry, and false assumptions.

Do you have family or friends who fall into that category?

Are you in a situation where you could take a vacation abroad, or plan a sabbatical of some kind, and take such a friend or family member with you? It is possible that friend or family member might find themselves won over to a new and better worldview by such an experience? And, if so, would you consider suggesting such an expedition?

If you yourself can't get away, is there merit in encouraging that friend or family member to travel? Are you in a position to persuade them to have an experience that might significantly change their worldview? (You don't have to state your agenda in doing so, of course; it will be good for them if you just make such a suggestion for its own sake.)

At the very least, it is a healthy and positive thing to do for ourselves. Consider taking your next vacation abroad, and make a point of capturing as much of your adventures in sharable format as possible – pics, videos, souvenirs and other artifacts of your experience. Then go out of your way to share them with the friends and family who could do with a little shake-up of their worldview. Tell personal stories about the people you met, what they were like, and the things you did together. Communicate the richness of your experience.

In advancing our embrace of diversity and pushing back against prejudice, even a little helps a lot.

"...and yesterday he didn't know the difference between a ship and a boat!"

Investigate!

On his final day at Gage Whitney, Sam has a lot to say. He's saying it in a conference room at the law firm, in front of his boss and representatives of an oil company for whom the firm is purchasing a cheap fleet of inadequate oil tankers. He tells the clients that he has an idea.[4]

"Instead of buying these ships - don't buy these ships. Buy other ships. Better ships. That's my idea."

"What is he talking about?" one of the oil executives asks.

"...and the good news is we have a no-penalty clause we can exercise if we pull out before the first of December!" Sam cheerfully adds.

"But Sam, we want these ships. This is as little as we've ever paid for a fleet."

"Well, there's a reason why they don't cost a lot of money. They're 20-year-old single hulled VLCCs that nobody wants!" Sam replies. "When they hit things, they will break. And they *will* hit things, because they don't have state-of-the-art

---

[4] In "In the Shadow of Two Gunmen", S2/E1.

navigation systems. They don't have G3 tank gauging, or EM-5000 engine monitoring, the recommended staletronic or electro-pneumatic ballast!"

Danny Concannon has just gotten back from Bermuda and is chatting with CJ in her office. He speaks as though sharing vacation adventures, but they both know he's talking about something else entirely.[5]

"I was riding into Hamilton when I saw a bunch of people playing cricket. And I like sports, though it turns out, not as much as I'd thought. But that's not the point."

"What was the point?"

"I met a guy there, a Bermudian whose name I'm not going to tell you right now. He was explaining the game to me. He's a cricket nut. He plays in a league. And he's a ramp signal agent at a small airstrip. He marshals planes as they're coming in. He was telling me a story to illustrate how much he loves cricket. There was a day his supervisor told his four-person crew they had tomorrow off 'cause a training crew was coming in to work their shift. Well, the next day, the guy realized that he left his cricket bat in his locker at work and his wife had the car so he walks six miles back to the airstrip to get it. Except, when he got there, he wasn't allowed in. Three men in coveralls, who identified themselves as being part of the training crew, were standing out front. All three of them were white, two of them had Southern accents.

"On May 21st, he was told to take tomorrow off. On the 22nd, Abdul Shareef's plane went off radar 85 miles from Bermuda."

"This is like something you'd get on the Internet," CJ says,

---

[5] In "Holy Night", S4/E11.

trying to sound dismissive.

"I'm back and I'm happy about it. And I think you know how I feel about you. But don't mess me around on this story, okay? The three guys out front were U.S. Army Rangers."

When the story everyone else accepts doesn't sound quite right - find out for yourself!

That's what Sam did when he realized everyone was buying into a bad idea, based on false assurances and bad assumptions. That's what Danny did, when Shareef's death seemed a little too convenient. Both of them dug in and started relentlessly pursuing the actual facts.

The Authoritarian relies on the masses to accept what they're told – by their own in-group, if not the population as a whole. The autocrat leverages this passive acceptance for his own purposes, and revels in how little effort is often required to sell a belief or an agenda that isn't supported by fact, simply by repeating it often to a group that will then bleat it out.

Never settle for that, not even from your own in-group. Certainly there are people we trust in our lives to inform us honestly and accurately, but it's such a good idea to develop personal investigation as our default, in processing what we learn about events around us.

"Figure things out for yourself," advised Timothy Snyder Spend more time with long articles. Subsidize investigative journalism by subscribing to print media. Realize that some of what is on the Internet is there to harm you. Learn about sites that investigate propaganda campaigns (some of which come from abroad). Take responsibility for what you communicate to others."

"'What is truth?' he goes on to ask. "Sometimes people ask this question because they wish to do nothing. Generic cynicism makes us feel hip and alternative even as we slip along with our fellow citizens into a morass of indifference. It is your ability to discern facts that makes you an individual, and our collective trust in common knowledge that makes us a society. The individual who investigates is also the citizen who builds. The leader who dislikes the investigators is a potential tyrant.

"If we do pursue the facts, the internet gives us enviable power to convey them. Leszek Kołakowski, the great Polish philosopher and historian, lost his chair at Warsaw University for speaking out against the communist regime, and could not publish. The first quotation in this book, from Hannah Arendt, came from a pamphlet entitled 'We Refugees', a miraculous achievement written by someone who had escaped a murderous Nazi regime. A brilliant mind like Victor Klemperer, much admired today, is remembered only because he stubbornly kept a hidden diary under Nazi rule. For him it was sustenance: 'My diary was my balancing pole, without which I would have fallen down a thousand times.'

He quotes others on the topic:

"If the main pillar of the system is living a lie," wrote Václav Havel, "then it is not surprising that the fundamental threat to it is living in truth."[6] Synder added, "Since in the age of the internet we are all publishers, each of us bears some private responsibility for the public's sense of truth. If we are serious about seeking the facts, we can each make a small revolution in the way the internet works. If you are verifying information for yourself, you will not send on fake news to others. If you choose to follow reporters whom you have reason to trust, you can also transmit what they have learned to others. If you retweet only the work of humans who have followed journalistic protocols, you are less likely to debase your brain interacting with bots and trolls. We do not see the minds that we hurt when we publish falsehoods, but that does not mean we do no harm."

And Hanna Arendt:

""Under normal circumstances the liar is defeated by reality, for which there is no substitute; no matter how large the tissue

---

[6] In the essay "The Power of the Powerless".

of falsehood that an experienced liar has to offer, it will never be large enough, even if he enlists the help of computers, to cover the immensity of factuality." ...to which Snyder added, "The part about computers is no longer true. For many Americans, the two-dimensional world of the internet has become more important than the three-dimensional world of human contact. People going door-to-door encounter the surprised blinking of American citizens who realize that they have to talk about politics with a flesh-and-blood human being rather than having their views affirmed by their Facebook feeds. Within the two-dimensional internet world, new collectivities have arisen, invisible by the light of day - tribes with distinct worldviews, beholden to manipulations."

Still, Arendt was making an important point about "the inherent power of facts to overcome falsehoods in a free society."

Arm yourself with facts, and gather them yourself.

"I like to read! They let me come early and stay after."

Be Well-Informed

A 19-year-old intern named Winnifred Hooper spanks Sam (so to speak) in front of Ed and Larry, correcting him on the contents and priority of a series of government reports he's dismissing as unimportant. How is she able to do that?[7]

"I've read the report," she explains.

"You've read the report?"

"I'm allowed. Anybody's allowed."

"So it just happens you read the report I pulled off the top?"

"I've read them all," she admits.

Sam and Ainsley are arguing about a summary Ainsley did of a position paper Sam wrote on white collar fraud, except she didn't summarize so much as she reversed his position.[8]

---

[7] In "The Stackhouse Filibuster", S2/E17.

[8] In "The Lame Duck Congress", S2/E6.

"I can't believe I'm listening to a Republican tell me the government should run background checks and impede business. In fact, I can't believe I'm listening to a Republican. Could it possibly be that most of the people you want to fingerprint have darker skin than you do?"

"Well, not to let the facts interfere with a good story, but 80% of violators are white. Fraudulent employees are three times more likely to be married, they're four times more likely to be to be men, 16 times more likely to be managers and executives and guess what, professor, they're five times more likely to have post graduate degrees."

"You, listen. I, you know, I can't. All right. Start from the beginning."

"Really?"

"Yeah."

"Are you eating that doughnut?"

"Take the doughnut. Start from the beginning."

Sam's experience is all too common, isn't it? When we think we already know, or accept the story others are accepting, we seldom go out of our way to inform ourselves further.

It's a natural human tendency. And the Authoritarian counts on it.

The cliché that "history is written by the winners" presents over and over again in our own. And the revisionists are, invariably, the winning autocrats: egalitarians understand history as collective heritage, prefer to base their future decisions on the trial-and-error learnings of the past – good and bad – and have no interest in living in lies.

"The belief that an informed citizenry is essential to the survival of American democracy is as old as the republic itself," wrote Richard Haass. "Thomas Jefferson emphasized the link, pointing out that 'wherever the people are well informed they can be trusted with their own government; that whenever things get so far wrong as to attract their notice, they may be relied on to set them to rights.' Some two centuries later, the forty-fourth president, Barack Obama, made a similar point, arguing that 'This democracy doesn't work if we don't have an informed citizenry.'"

The admonitions of Jefferson and Obama notwithstanding, the US has been by no means exempt from the consequences of poorly-informed citizens. Efforts by those who insist on being well-informed, and helping others to be as well, can rise to the level of the heroic.

A relatively recently example in the American story is the story of Daniel Ellsberg, a journalist and analyst who, after eyewitnessing the escalating conflict in Vietnam in the Sixties, photocopied secure documents locked away at the RAND Corporation, where he later worked. The documents were massive reports compiled by Robert McNamara, former Secretary of Defense under Presidents Kennedy and Johnson, summarizing the true history of the Vietnam conflict. They documented extensive falsehoods foisted upon the American public by half a dozen presidential administrations, including those of Kennedy, Johnson, and Nixon; the war was, in fact, hopeless, they had known it for years, and president after president kept sending American boys to die anyway.

Ellsberg, having seen this for himself, decided the public needed to be as well-informed as he was; so he leaked the documents, which came to be known as the Pentagon Papers, to journalist Neil Sheehan of the *New York Times*. The *Times* and the *Washington Post* published them for all to see, inspiring rage in the Nixon White House, triggering a Supreme Court showdown – and bringing tremendous persecution to Ellsberg's doorstep.

It was the right thing to do, and it caused great furor – but it also changed the course of American history. Public outcry led to the long-overdue cessation of US military action in Vietnam.

"Why is an informed citizenry essential?" Haass asked.

"American democracy is a representative (rather than direct) democracy, in which citizens do not make day-to-day decisions as to what the federal, state, or local government should do with its powers and resources but rather elect individuals to do just that. It is thus a republic; in the words of James Madison, 'a government which derives all its powers directly or indirectly from the great body of the people, and is administered by persons holding their offices during pleasure, for a limited period, or during good behavior.' The obvious reason, then, for citizens to be informed is to be able to wisely cast their votes. In almost every instance there are two or more candidates vying for a position, and it is in your self-interest to know enough to determine which of the candidates would be likely to advance or support policies you judge to be desirable. Implicit in this decision is knowing not simply what a candidate stands for but also the likely consequences of the policies they stand for and oppose so that you are in a position to determine what policy choices make the most sense."

Be Winnifred Hooper. Be Sam and Ainsley. Dig up the facts, put them on the table. Find the truth - and raise up your voice, whenever you must, to set the record straight.

"...not that polished communication skills are an important part of this job!"

Make Smart Use of Language

Trapped in Southern Indiana, Josh and Toby while away their exile in endless rumination over the campaign of President Bartlet's opponent in the upcoming election – noting, in particular, that Gov. Rob Ritchie is not particularly well-spoken:[9]

"And I don't care about the Greco-Roman wrestling matches with the language," Toby rants, "-not that polished communication skills are an important part of this job! What I care about is when he was asked if he'd continue the current US policy in China he said, 'First off, I'm going to send them a message - meet an American leader.' I don't know what that means, but everybody cheered!"

Anticipating the upcoming breakfast with Congressional leadership – a purely ceremonial exercise – the senior staff is

---

[9] In "20 Hours in America", S4/E1.

obsessing over negotiations with the majority leader's chief of staff over topics to be allowed and language to be used.

"I see we won't be talking about the 993 tax cut," Josh notes.

"We won't be," Leo confirms. "But we've agreed to call it 'tax relief' instead of a tax cut."

"We're calling it 'tax relief'."

"Yeah."

"But we won't be talking about it."

"No."

"Leo, the Patient's Bill of Rights-"

"-which we'll be referring to as the Comprehensive Access and Responsibility Act. The Republicans have agreed to discuss changing the name back."

"In exchange for calling tax breaks 'tax relief'."

"I'm in a musical," Toby declares.

Lots going on here, and all of it deeply relevant to the threat of Authoritarianism.

First is the issue of *framing* – exploiting words and phrases to control public discourse by crafting a context around them that triggers certain ideas in the mind of the listener.

Then there's the conscious mobilization of language itself to usurp social and cultural control. The US political right has been doing this for decades.

Finally, the Authoritarian uses a particular set of words that are giveaways, if we know to listen for them.

Let's look at each of these.

Use your words!

The ease with which the senior staff concedes to using Republican language – and President Bartlet's repeated displays of indifference to what things are called, in various episodes – are *huge* mistakes. Republicans are masterful at a skill that is a popular go-to in the Authoritarian playbook: *framing*.

Berkeley cognitive scientist George Lakoff is the pacesetter in this area, beginning with his book *Metaphors We Live By*, which suggested that we build our internal models of the world out of frameworks driven by concepts about reality that we've absorbed, and expand our understanding by assigning meaning sitting in one frame to the new frames we build.

Put another way, when we hear or experience something new, we will subconsciously push toward an understanding of it by dropping it into a frame we already possess.

Example:

Argument is **war**

This metaphor takes the concept of *argument* and drops it into the *war* frame I possess. If I take this metaphor on board, then I will assign the features of *war* to my understanding of *argument*: war is conflict; there is a winner and a loser; the idea is to defeat the other person. Argument, in this metaphor, becomes conflict, and the objective is to defeat the other.

Then again:

Argument is **dance**

This metaphor works the same way, but in assigning a different frame, it imbues *argument* with different features: when two people dance, there is move and countermove; there is cooperation; there is synchronization, in varying degrees; and there is a shared goal. Viewed within the *dance* frame, *argument* becomes altogether different.

Lakoff isn't just a language expert; he's also a political activist, authoring *The Political Mind* and *Don't Think of an Elephant!*, two books that bring this framing concept into the realm of politics, where it is leveraged to high heaven. Political rhetoric oozes framing language, and it is used to steer our thinking without our realizing it.

Example, from Lakoff:

"Take "tax relief," a phrase used by the current White House [Bush II]. The word *relief* evokes a conceptual frame of some affliction - an afflicted party, and a reliever who performs the action of relieving. So taxes are an affliction, a reliever is a hero, and anyone who wants to stop him from the relief is a villain. You have just two words, yet all of that is embedded. If you oppose reducing taxes and you use that phrase - *tax relief* - you've already lost."

Put another way,

"For there to be relief, there must be an affliction, an afflicted party, and a reliever who removes the affliction and is therefore a hero. And if people try to stop the hero, those people are villains for trying to prevent relief. When the word tax is added to relief, the result is a metaphor: Taxation is an affliction. And the person who takes it away is a hero, and anyone who tries to stop him is a bad guy. This is a frame. It is made up of ideas, like affliction and hero."

And here's another Lakoff example quoting Bush II:

Another example Lakoff mentions in his book is when Bush proclaimed in his State of the Union address in January 2005 that "we do not need a permission slip to defend America." Consider what Bush is saying here. Sure, he could have said, "we won't ask permission," but saying "permission slip" evokes the adult-child metaphor, which aligns with conservatives' strict father worldview, according to Lakoff.

The Republicans weren't always so savvy about framing. Lakoff is fond of pointing out that when Nixon got on television and stated, *"I am not a crook!"*, he was foolishly invoking a frame that doomed him: now Americans could see him as nothing *but* a crook.

In the years since, Republicans have come to understand framing thoroughly; they not only actively practice it incessantly (for decades now), but write playbooks about it.

Newt Gingrich, for instance, when planning his conservative resurgence in Congress in the early Nineties, he wrote a memo that was distributed to Republican officeholders entitled "Language: A Key Mechanism of Control".

"In it, he carried on from Joseph Goebbels, who had repeatedly asserted that in order to control a society, one must first take control of that society's language. Gingrich gave Republicans a list of words to describe anything having to do with Democrats," wrote Thom Hartmann in *The Hidden History of American Oligarchy*:

decay, failure (fail), collapse(ing), deeper, crisis, urgent(cy), destructive, destroy, sick, pathetic, lie, liberal, they/them, unionized bureaucracy, "compassion" is not enough, betray, consequences, limit(s), shallow, traitors, sensationalists, endanger, coercion, hypocrisy, radical, threaten, devour, waste, corruption, incompetent, permissive attitude, destructive, impose, self-serving, greed, ideological, insecure, anti-(issue): flag, family, child, jobs; pessimistic, excuses, intolerant, stagnation, welfare, corrupt, selfish, insensitive, status quo, mandate(s) taxes, spend (ing) shame, disgrace, punish (poor . . .), bizarre, cynicism, cheat, steal, abuse of power, machine, bosses, obsolete, criminal rights, red tape, patronage.

"Gingrich told Republicans that it was as important to characterize themselves in a positive light as it was to trash-talk Democrats. His list of words to apply to themselves and their policies was as follows," Hartmann continued:

share, change, opportunity, legacy, challenge, control, truth, moral, courage, reform, prosperity, crusade, movement, children, family, debate, compete, active(ly), we/us/our, candid(ly), humane, pristine, provide, liberty, commitment, principle(d), unique, duty, precious, premise, care(ing), tough, listen, learn, help, lead, vision, success, empower(ment), citizen, activist, mobilize, conflict, light, dream, freedom, peace, rights, pioneer, proud/pride, building, preserve, pro-(issue): flag, children, environment; reform, workfare, eliminate good-time in prison, strength, choice/choose, fair, protect, confident, incentive, hard work, initiative, common sense, passionate.

"When tyranny begins to emerge, shifts in language become obvious, and it's important to pay close attention to how language is used, especially when certain phrases or memes are used repeatedly," Hartmann wrote. "Tyrants understand that it's more important to control the news than to control the army; armies will follow what they believe to be true, but only when first convinced of its truth, and that requires control of or substantial influence over the news."

So blatant is this manipulative usage that it is now a standard practice among Republican lawmakers to simply name things the opposite of what they really are, in order to have them accepted: *The Clear Skies Initiative! No Child Left Behind!*□

Both Lakoff and Hartmann have spent years trying to get Democratic leaders to take this message seriously and to realize that they are only hurting themselves by submitting to their opponents' framing, rather than developing their own.

Bill Clinton was the exception, Lakoff noted: he understood framing and how to make it work, not just for him, but against his opposition.

"He stole the other side's language," Lakoff wrote. "He walked about 'welfare reform', for example. He said, 'The age of big government is over.' He did what he wanted to do, only he took their language and used their words to describe it. It made them very mad."

Overtures to both the Obama team and Hillary Clinton team were dismissed, Lakoff has lamented. Either the psychology itself wasn't being taken seriously, or the use of framing as a method of political persuasion was being interpreted as manipulation.

But is it? Doesn't every effective speechwriter, regardless of their political leaning, employ exactly these techniques? Didn't Lincoln? Didn't JFK and King? Framing is simply science; it's how human brains work. Is it out-of-bounds to employ it inaccurately get one's message across?

Lakoff summarizes frames as "mental structures that shape the way we see the world." They are neither left nor right; they're simply there. And we are all carrying around many frames, often covering the same domain; it isn't manipulation to take care to use words that steer your message into the frame you intend. It's stupid, in fact, not to.

A final point, this one from Hartmann: liberals try to engage the mind, while conservatives try to engage emotions; liberals talk facts, conservatives tell stories. The intuitive advantage of the conservative messaging is that human brains become emotionally engaged first, intellectually engaged thereafter; and the human brain's ancient roots are in storytelling, while recitation of fact is relatively new in history. Liberals, then, are employing a losing strategy when they fail to learn from how conservatives communicate.

It's not tough to learn these principles and commit to them; and it's long past time the left got its act together, and started truly using their words.

What to listen for

From Snyder: "Victor Klemperer, a literary scholar of Jewish origin, turned his philological training against Nazi propaganda. He noticed how Hitler's language rejected legitimate opposition: The people always meant some people and not others (an American president said *my people*), encounters were always struggles (an American variant is *winning*), and any attempt to understand the world in a different way was defamation of the leader (or, as an American president put it, *treason*).

"Politicians in our times feed their clichés to television, where even those who wish to disagree repeat them. Television purports to challenge political language by conveying images, but the succession from one frame to another can hinder a sense of resolution. Everything happens fast, but nothing actually happens. Each story on televised news is "breaking" until it is displaced by the next one. So we are hit by wave upon wave but never see the ocean."

"Listen for dangerous words," Snyder went on to advise: "Be alert to the use of the words *extremism* and *terrorism*. Be alive to the fatal notions of *emergency* and *exception*. Be angry about the treacherous use of patriotic vocabulary."

And from Mycielski:

"They will distort the language, coin new terms and labels, repeat shocking phrases until you accept them as normal and subconsciously associate them with whom they like. A "thief", "liar" or "traitor" will automatically mean the opposition, while a "patriot" or a "true American" will mean their follower (see point 2). Their slogans will have double meaning, giving strength to their supporters and instilling angst in their opponents. *Fight changes in language in the public sphere, remind and preserve the true meaning of words.*"

Finally, there's the lesson of Rob Ritchie: in political speech, it's not so much the content of a politician's message that sways voters; it's the emotions their words bring to the surface, even if the words are nonsensical. We've certainly seen plenty of truth in that in recent US politics.

"In a country born on a will to be free, what could be more fundamental than this?"

Protect Your Privacy!

Peyton Cabot Harrison is the Bartlet Administration's pick to replace retiring Supreme Court Justice Joseph Crouch, but Sam has been tipped off that Harrison once expressed in a law paper that he does not believe the Constitution supports a right to privacy. This is a big red flag for President Bartlet. Harrison is brought to the Oval Office for a conversation about it. Sure enough, Harrison's position on privacy is that the government has a right to invade it.[10]

"It's about the next 20 years," Sam underscores, when speaking alone with Toby and the President. "Twenties and Thirties, it was the role of government. Fifties and Sixties, it was civil rights. The next two decades, it's gonna be privacy. I'm talking about the Internet. I'm talking about cellphones. I'm talking about health records, and who's gay and who's

---

[10] In "The Short List", S1/E9.

not. And moreover, in a country born on a will to be free, what could be more fundamental than this?"

Privacy is one of the greatest issues and challenges we face, rising Authoritarianism aside. In the age of the cell phone, Internet, social media, and machine learning, it's difficult to know where to even start in considering and addressing how threats to our privacy affect us – let alone what we should do about them.

When we add Authoritarianism to the mix, seeing how our personal information can be turned against us, the issue feels openly oppressive.

"What the great political thinker Hannah Arendt meant by totalitarianism was not an all-powerful state, but the erasure of the difference between private and public life," wrote Timothy Synder. "We are free only insofar as we exercise control over what people know about us, and in what circumstances they come to know it."

Our personal privacy can be violated in a number of ways that compromise our well-being and safety, both individually and collectively:

- **Personal ID information.** Too much identifying information makes us easier to track and hack.
- **Health information.** Information about our personal health or health history can be exploited to our financial and career disadvantage. That's why HIPAA regulations are in place today, and why deregulating personal health information would be desirable to the Authoritarian.
- **Ethnicity and sexuality.** Disclosure of personal details about our ethnicity and sexual orientation can be used to have us targeted for discrimination, or even make us sought out by hate groups.
- **Social media expression.** Many if not most of us express ourselves regularly on social media, and

reveal details about our lives, our opinions, our backgrounds. All of this information is exploitable, in the wrong hands.

- **Harvested self-expression in machine learning.** That same social media data, as well as more private information (such as health and financial records) can – even if anonymous – be bundled with the data of thousands of other people and folded into machine learning processes, creating powerful and unregulated AI, which can be used for a broad array of dark purposes useful to the Authoritarian.

"Nastier rulers will use what they know about you to push you around," wrote Timothy Snyder. "If we have no control over who reads what and when, we have no ability to act in the present or plan for the future. Whoever can pierce your privacy can humiliate you and disrupt your relationships at will. No one (except perhaps a tyrant) has a private life that can survive public exposure by hostile directive."

The uncomfortable truth is that most of us are pretty free and easy with our online lives. We leave big trails of private information behind us wherever we go in cyberspace, and essentially fill out exhaustively detailed profiles of ourselves as we go – profiles that are easily accessed by those who know how. The more information about ourselves we exude, the more vulnerable we are to threat or manipulation by the Authoritarian. And we can do something about that.

Buttoning Up Our Lives

By taking very deliberate steps to protect our personal privacy, and by encouraging our friends and family members to do the same, we take a giant step back from the encroaching autocrat. We make it that much harder for they to control us, to exploit us, to threaten us. We are safer; they are spread more thinly, the more of us there are who take such steps.

Here are some of those steps:

- **Passwords.** Take password security *very* seriously; hacking in this domain has become deeply sophisticated. Many sites and apps require highly complex passwords. Go with it.[11]
- **Two-factor authentication.** Having to authenticate twice rather than once to open an app or gain access to a web page is a pain, it's true; but adding a spontaneously-generated access code to a password requirement doesn't just double the security – it bumps it up exponentially.
- **Public wi-fi.** There are few environments more unsafe than public wi-fi. Those who make use of public wi-fi, even just to check email, are running a big risk of having their laptop or tablet compromised, offering access to account information, etc. Public wi-fi should only be used for the most innocuous purposes, when other security measures are in place to protect information on the device being used.
- **Anti-virus software.** Use it, make sure it's high-quality, and make sure you take the updates, as improvements address the latest threats.
- **Privacy settings on apps and websites.** Many apps and websites offer the user control over what data may and may not be shared. Take the time to review these options when they are

---

[11] This seems intimidating at times, but can be fun; for instance, you can create a password from a phrase you'll never forget: **Tbgw-1hgb4!** ("To boldly go where no one has gone before!"

offered, and make prudent choices.

- **Cookies and other browser trackers.** Many if not most companies want to put cookies on your device. This allows them to track your activity, not just when using their apps and visiting their sites, but to map your trail to other sites. They do this to create buying behavioral analytics. Profitable for them, potentially invasive for you.

- **Do personal in person.** It's a wise policy, not just with regard to online habits but in life generally, to have personal exchanges in person. Safer, from a privacy standpoint, and healthier, from a human one.

- **Need to know.** Don't self-disclose casually on social media unless the subject matter is truly innocuous. Only put information online that others really need to know. Get in the habit of asking yourself before hitting Enter.

- **Learn about online scams.** There are many effective scams in play, all over the digital universe. Many are email-related, intending to bait the user into giving up hackable knowledge. Learn what these are and how to avoid them.

- **Private web browser.** Just as cookies planted in your machine make your online activity trackable, so some browsers track your activity for marketing and ad-targeting purposes. But your digital footprints also reveal other information about you, so it's best to leave no trail at all. Consider a private web browser like DuckDuckGo or Ecosia.

- **Opt-out on demographic details.** Many online forms and questionnaires provide users with the option of omitting various demographic details about themselves. It's a good default to opt out of any revelation of demographic detail that isn't essential.

The Authoritarian threats made possible through privacy invasions are serious, even potentially grave, Snyder warned.

"Scrub your computer of malware on a regular basis," he advised. "Remember that email is skywriting. Consider using alternative forms of the internet, or simply using it less. Have personal exchanges in person. For the same reason, resolve any legal trouble. Tyrants seek the hook on which to hang you. Try not to have hooks."

"You really want to reach in and kill them where they live? Keep accepting more than one idea. Makes 'em absolutely crazy!"

Pluralist societies vs. Ideological regimes

A group of high school kids are visiting the West Wing when a precautionary lockdown occurs, due to a terrorism alert. The staff are used to such events, which have become a mere inconvenience, but to reassure the students, they take turns discussing the situation in the world with them.[12]

The subject turns to the causes of terrorism – political and religious extremism, in particular. Josh takes the ball:

"What's Islamic extremism? It's strict adherence to a particular interpretation of 7th century Islamic law as practiced by the prophet Mohammed," he tells the kids, "and when I say 'strict adherence,' I'm not kidding around. Men are forced to pray, wear their beards a certain length. Among my

---

[12] In "Isaac and Ishmael", S3/E0.

favorites is there's only one acceptable cheer at a soccer match: *'Allah-uh-Akbar'*: 'God is great.' If your guys are getting creamed, then you're on your own.

"Things are a lot less comic for women, who aren't allowed to attend school or have jobs. They're not allowed to be unaccompanied, and oftentimes get publicly stoned to death for crimes like not wearing a veil. I don't have to tell you they don't need to shout at a soccer match because they're never going to go to one.

"So what bothers them about us? Well, the variety of cheers alone coming from the cheap seats at Giants stadium when they're playing the Cowboys is enough for a jihad, to say nothing of street corners lined church next to synagogue, next to mosque; newspapers that can print anything they want; women who can do anything they want, including taking a rocket ship to outer space, vote, and play soccer.

"This is a plural society. That means we accept more than one idea. It offends them."

Josh's speech here is the keynote for the episode – a summary surrounding a complex and long-standing problem in human history, not just US security, but one that almost every society has confronted at one time or another: what happens when worldviews collide. His answer – accept more than one worldview – is more poignant and profound than even he fully realizes.

In the era of the nation's founding, Western civilization had already been through considerable rise-and-fall of various paradigms of societal rule: monarchy, autocracy, tyranny; religious, philosophical, elitist governance. All had their bad points; some had their good points.

But they all had one thing in common: one worldview was dominant; other worldviews were suppressed. Why? Because in those earlier social/political structures, one person or one class ruled everyone else. And within those structures, different worldviews were a threat to those in power.

The Founders realized that this didn't have to be; that it must be possible to create a nation of self-governing people, after the example of the Roman Republic, where those who ruled were drawn not from society's elites, but from all quarters. Jed Bartlet said it like this:

"My great-grandfather's great-grandfather was Dr. Josiah Bartlet, who was the New Hampshire delegate to the second Continental Congress, the one that sat in session in Philadelphia in the summer of 1776, and announced to the world that we were no longer subjects of King George III, but rather a self-governing people. We hold these truths to be self-evident, they said, that all men are created equal. Strange as it may seem, that was the first time in history that anyone had bothered to write that down. Decisions are made by those who show up."

A self-governing people – where everyone had a voice. Where multiple worldviews were welcome. Where the idea of one-worldview-rules-all – the paradigm of the nation that their parents had left behind insisted on – need not be their societal rule.

Of course, it was an incomplete idea, as the Founders themselves hadn't yet wrapped their minds around the idea that women are as smart and capable as men, or that how much property one owns doesn't really matter – but the general principle, that it's okay if people think differently, was woven into the core of their ambition. The United States would be a nation whose citizens were free – free to think what they please, say what they please, and see the world as they please.

Pluralism.

Not being an anthropologist, we can safely assume that Josh Lyman didn't fully realize that the idea of free thinking and multiple worldviews in society and government may have been the exception in Western history, but not in all of human history.

Cognitive diversity is actually the inevitable human condition. Our social and political biases are, to some degree, learned from those around us – the families we grow up in, the friends who surround us – but they are also largely a result of our cognitive tendencies, and those tendencies are genetic.

Some people are risk-takers; some are risk-averse. Some people find comfort in routine and sameness, while others enjoy the excitement of change, in the new-and-different. Some people see the safety and progress of their community as best decided by consensus, while others feel safest when someone powerful is in charge.

And because these tendencies are genetic, we'll find all of these people in every society, every human population. Today, yesterday, and in the distant past.

Before civilization – before structured societies and government – we lived in nomadic tribes. And that great diversity in thinking and viewpoint is what kept us alive. We needed the risk-takers, the novelty-seekers, the ones who could head out into the woods or the plains and come back with food. And we needed, every bit as much, the fire-tenders – those people who were cautious, more afraid than others, who were perfectly willing to sit by the fire at night and keep it burning bright, to scare away predators.

If we'd all been risk-takers, we'd never have lasted. And if we'd all been fire-tenders, we'd never have lasted. And not just those two types, but all types. Human diversity in cognition is as deep and powerful, if not more, as human physical and social diversity.

Pluralism is why we're alive. It's why we thrive. And when we cluster into this likeminded group or that, from religions to political parties, we severely limit that ability to thrive.

The Founders gave us a structure, a nation, that could thrive – a government where many ways of thinking were welcome, and processes that allowed everyone to put their ideas out there for consideration without any one person or group dominating the others. Where it was the ideas, not the person or the group, that ultimately became the basis for action.

It's no exaggeration to claim that the Founders' template for human progress represents a decisive return to the societal framework that sustained us for almost 3,000 centuries.

In the here-and-now, 20-plus years beyond Josh's speech and Bartlet's history lesson, the Founders' vision is more under threat than ever.

The United States hasn't been as polarized, as divided, as it is in the 2020s since the Civil War. It's Red and Blue, through and through, with each side seeing the other as existential threat.

At this writing, in the summer of 2024, the GOP is led by MAGA and Donald Trump, and is making no secret of its intention to eliminate democracy in the US altogether (see: Project 2025). The mutual demonization between Right and Left is all we see anymore.

Even SCOTUS Justice Samuel Alito spoke the words (although unknowingly) when he told filmmaker Lauren Windsor (who was recording him) in June of 2024, "One side or the other is going to win."

"I mean, there can be a way of working — a way of living together peacefully," he went on to say, "but it's difficult, you know, because there are differences on fundamental things that really can't be compromised. They really can't be compromised."

No, Justice Alito, there is no "winning"; neither side can ever "win". Both sides will always be there. For one side to "win", to take control and dominate US society, culture, and governance, is to suppress and control all the other sides. And then we're back to England 1750. We won't be the United States anymore.

Josh is right: we need to have more than one idea. We must *always* accept more than one idea. We must accept that seeing things differently is our natural state, and granting each other that freedom is our natural obligation, and that our path forward must be founded on exactly that which Alito eschews: *compromise*. We have our differences, inevitable differences, but that's as it should be. That's human nature. It's a survival tool we can't do without.

Those who want one-party rule or extremist ideology in place to control a population aren't just despotic; they are holding a gun to their own heads. If one side "wins," that's the ball game. We *need* differences to thrive; we *need* the art of compromise in our societal toolkit, in order to forge the path that's truly best for all.

So – *accept more than one idea...*

"We're gonna listen to the experts."

Respect Science and Experience

The White House staff's respect for CJ is, of course, well-earned. Press Secretary is one of the toughest jobs in all of politics, and those who hold the post must constantly walk a tightrope with no net – and there's a pool of piranha on one side and a velociraptor pen on the other.

The White House Press Room is where the world gets its clearest indication of what a president is thinking and who the president is listening to, based on what the press secretary passes along. And one specific domain of thought and deference has risen above all others in recent years: a president's respect for scientific truth.

The threat of the coronavirus pandemic loomed large. And the parade of misinformation, disinformation and outright bullshit that has issued forth from the Trump White House press room was staggering.

In fairness, that press room has seen less activity than any other administration in modern history, and one doesn't need any of its many press secretaries to know what Trump is thinking – all one needs is a Twitter account. But the questions of who a president listens to and whether or not we know about it are all the more pressing for the Trump Administration's disinterest in the views of experts.

When is it okay to lie from the podium?

As it turns out, the Bartlet White House isn't sinless when it comes to misleading the press. It happened for the first time when the CIA was caught napping as a massive armed confrontation between Indian and Pakistani troops suddenly erupted, and Bartlet and Leo and Toby elected to keep CJ out of the loop initially – sending her into the press room, for all practical purposes, to lie. Toby tried to smooth it over...

"I was warned that coming to talk to you might be insulting to your professionalism," he says upon entering her office.

"Well, you wouldn't want to do that." She's clearly still very pissed.

"I wasn't ready for the press yet," he says, as if that makes anything better.

"Could've told me that before sending me in there," she replies.

"CJ-"

"I flatly denied it," she says, cutting him off. "I said I was in the Oval Office ten minutes ago and nothing's going on."

"They don't think you lied to them."

"I know that," she answers. "They think you lied to me, which is what happened. They don't know me. I'm from nowhere. I was just starting to get credible. I was just starting to get their respect. You know how long it's going to take me to get it back?"

"There's a concern-"

"'Don't ask CJ, she doesn't know anything!'"

"-there is a concern that you're too friendly with the press."

"Really."

"We know it's important that you have a friendly relationship with them-"

"It's important for all of us!"

"I don't disagree."

"Does this have to do with Danny Concannon?"

"People see you with Danny-"

"This is outrageous!"

"This is one time, and if we erred, it's on the side of trying to-"

"You sent me in there uninformed so that I'd lie to the press-"

"We sent you in there uninformed because we thought there was a chance you couldn't."

Is it ever okay to lie to the press?

In the scene above, the consensus of Bartlet and Leo and Toby was that they needed to stall on speaking on the record about the India-Pakistan confrontation until they knew more about what was happening and had time to plan their response. For CJ to get the question and tell the truth would have been politically disastrous, eroding confidence in the White House for purely circumstantial reasons. Such a lie is ethically gray, but understandable.

Lying to the press for political reasons is one thing; what about changing the story when it's science, rather than politics, that are at stake?

Science denial isn't just routine in the US at this point; it seems to be a plank in the GOP platform. And taking an anti-science stance from a White House podium isn't simply failing to be forthcoming; it erodes public confidence in professional expertise. That goes beyond the moment – it can do lasting damage.

Leo himself indulges in this editing of science, having his own showdown with CJ Will Bailey reveals to the two of them that Reuters has a story saying that the White House deleted two paragraphs from an EPA report on energy usage because the language was critical of the coal industry.[13]

Leo tells Will and CJ that it was he who cut the paragraphs.

---

[13] In "Constituency of One", S5/E5.

CJ wants to back-pedal it, but Leo stands firm: "'The report will reflect administration views.' That's the line."

CJ gets the question in the next press briefing.

"Sources at the EPA say the White House censored language from a report critical of coal-based energy. Does the White House feel that's appropriate?"

"The White House feels the EPA report will reflect administration views," CJ dutifully replies.

"Not the EPA's views. Their draft cited stunted trees, poisoned fish and wildlife as just some of the problems with coal. Hasn't this president always-"

"The final report will lay out views on a range of issues."

"Why did the White House tamper with an independent report?"

"I've addressed that."

"No, you haven't. Why is all independent analysis subject to White House censorship?"

"I don't accept your premise."

"Doesn't the EPA have the right-"

"I'm sure you all look forward to reading the actual report."

"I've read both drafts, the censored one and the original. Are you defending-"

"If there was interference with an independent report, that was obviously a mistake."

CJ, surfing for dear life toward a beach she doesn't want to be on, has now incurred Leo's wrath.

"They had both drafts," she explains to Leo later. "There was nothing I could do."

"I gave you the line. Who said you could drop it?"

They proceed to argue over "clean coal," which CJ considers mythical, but Leo defends on the basis of less environmentally harmful byproducts.

"When I give you the line, that's the line," he says definitively.

"Not when no one will believe it."

"You're going to put out a statement in your own name," he

declares. "It's going to say what you should have said in that briefing room, that we stand behind that report."

"That's saying I wasn't speaking for this White House," she replies.

"You weren't," he says. "On my desk within the hour."

Ouch.

A War on Science

"Although scientific input to the government is rarely the only factor in public policy decisions, this input should always be weighed from an objective and impartial perspective to avoid perilous consequences. Indeed, this principle has long been adhered to by presidents and administrations of both parties in forming and implementing policies. The administration of George W. Bush has, however, disregarded this principle."

~"Restoring Scientific Integrity in Policymaking", the Union of Concerned Scientists

The Right in the US has been growing steadily more Authoritarian since Goldwater – and science isn't the Authoritarian's friend. Social dominance is about emotion, and facts are very inconvenient when emotions are at stake.

The GOP's pushback against science, learned testimony and professional expertise began with Reagan, when deregulation was the main course of the Right's legislative agenda and those pesky scientific experts kept introducing inconvenient facts into deregulation proceedings. But the GOP's anti-science penchant really hit its stride in 2001, with the Bush II administration.

While by no means the instigator of the Bush anti-science agenda, White House Science Advisor John Marburger was certainly its most visible exponent of it. It was he who responded to the Union of Concerned Scientists when they issued the document quoted above. That document, signed by more than 60 scientists and officials, highlighted the administration's systematic distortions of information, suppression of reports, and ideological selectivity in advisory panel appointments. It was a damning document, underscoring that the Bush White House represented a new low in the dismantling of professional expertise in policymaking.

Chris Mooney documents the clash between Marburger and his UCS critics in 2005's *The Republican War on Science*, a fact-packed, penetrating disclosure of the Right's steady erosion of public faith in the integrity of science for political ends. He lists luminaries Paul Ehrlich, E.O. Wilson and Republican environmentalist Russell Train among the UCS signatories, and details egregious, persistent malfeasance in the Bush White House's handling of scientific input into policy questions.

This malfeasance included modifications to the Endangered Species Act that made it harder to formally classify species and habitats in peril, over the objections of biologists; the jaw-dropping (and, in hindsight, outlandish) assertion that there was a connection between abortion and breast cancer; and documentation of the administration's cherry-picking of advisory panelists, based on their friendliness to conservative doctrine.

Marburger – a scientist himself, and a good one – became the public face of the Bush White House in responding to the UCS, whose missive had made its way to every major news outlet. His replies were not those of a scientist, however, but a spinner - laced with evasions, missed points, and furtive misdirection. The UCS, for its part, grew louder, and found allies in Congress willing to sound the alarm – including

Congressman Henry Waxman, who characterized the Bush Administration's manipulations as "nothing more than the political creation of scientific uncertainty."

The most egregious of Marburger's sins, in the harsh light of history, was his politicization of climate science, which artfully blurred the uncertainty lines by illuminating actual uncertainties about climate change while completely failing to mention the strong consensual conclusions of the scientific community. In this, he was following his boss's lead, but it put the lie to his perpetual claim that he was just a messenger – certainly *not* a spinner! - and his denials that he had any trace of a partisan agenda

"Such flagrant misrepresentation goes far beyond mere dishonesty," wrote Mooney. "It demonstrates a gross disregard for the welfare of the American public, who Bush represent[ed], and for the population of the entire globe, whose fate depends in large measure on the behavior of the American behemoth."

In late 2004, the *Washington Post* reported that the Bush White House had endeavored to suppress the Arctic Climate Impact Assessment, the scientific work of eight collaborating nations, with 300 participating scientists, and that it had "repeatedly resisted even mild language that would endorse the report's scientific findings."

The effects of the Bush White House assault on science remain to this day, of course; even a pro-science Democratic president like Barack Obama faced a confused, untrusting public, making the justification of sound policy all the more difficult.

Obama's Pandemics

Presidential dismissal or downplaying of scientific expertise over climate change (or any other public policy issue, for that matter) is certainly foolish, but it's not hard to see why much of the public lets it pass; though the long-term consequences are catastrophic (perhaps even existential), they are years, perhaps decades in the future. Even the near-term impact fails to register in the minds of many; climate change is, to a large degree, abstract. It's hard for some people to be afraid of what they can't see in front of them.

Public health risks are another matter. Pandemics, for instance, are both immediate and all too visible, as the world is learning as of this writing; the consequences are all around us, in the deaths of those afflicted, the daily barrage of media attention, the all-pervasive reminders like masks and hand sanitizer. If we drop that immediacy and threat into the mix with the conditions already mentioned – political expediency and the often-uncomfortable inconvenience of scientific fact – we're in a whole new territory.

And pandemics are just the highest-profile of the many public health concerns that present these days. Whether the threat is large or small, the question remains: Is it permissible, or even conscionable, to deny science and the advice of medical experts when public health is at stake?

The West Wing tackled this one in "Ellie", an episode focusing on President Bartlet's middle daughter, a medical student. After Dr. Millicent Griffith, the Surgeon General and a Bartlet family friend, says in an Internet interview that marijuana does not pose the same health risks as tobacco or alcohol, a firestorm erupts all around her, as this statement is at odds with the Bartlet Administration's negative stance on legalization. Matters become worse when Ellie Bartlet publicly comes to Griffith's defense: "My father won't fire the Surgeon General. He would never do that."

Now the president is fighting battles on two fronts: dealing with the political fallout from Dr. Griffith's apparent contradiction of administration policy, and what he perceives as his daughter sticking her nose into politics where it doesn't belong. Dealing with the former problem, Josh Lyman pays Griffith a visit and asks her to resign. She refuses; if the president wants her gone, he'll have to fire her.

After the jaw-dropping behavior of the Bush Administration, the pro-science openness of the Obama years was all too welcome.

"The good news is that President Barack Obama's administration, with a Nobel laureate as secretary of energy, a restored White House science adviser, and many other distinguished researchers in positions of major influence, represents a dramatic step forward for science and its role in public life," wrote Chris Mooney in 2009, the year Obama took office. "The 'reality-based community' has been reinstated in Washington; after the Bush administration and its 'war on science,' it feels like a sunrise. Yet we can't expect the long-standing gap between scientists and the broader American public to disappear overnight, meaning this is no time for satisfaction or complacency. If the metaphorical 'war' on science is over, now's the time for the long and difficult process of 'nation building' - for laying sounder foundations to ensure it doesn't come raging back." (Little did he know!)

The Obama Administration was terrific on accurately framing climate issues with scientific integrity. Creating and implementing a Climate Change Action Plan in coordination with the 2015 Paris Agreement that united more than 200 countries in a commitment to address climate change, it was the culmination of years of effort not only to focus the nation's considerable federal resources on the problem, but to engage the cooperation of mayors, governors, and businesses in the mission. It followed Obama's participation in the Copenhagen Accord (2009) and his administration's 2014 partnership with China in committing to reducing greenhouse gas emissions long-term.

Obama's science advisor, John Holdren, was a climate change firebrand, in contrast to Marburger. A MacArthur Fellow with a Stanford doctorate in aerospace engineering and theoretical plasma physics, he came to the White House post with a bulging portfolio, having published on climate change policy in *Scientific American*[87] and with the Brookings

Institute. He had previously served as a science advisor to Bill Clinton, and took over as Director of the Office of Science and Technology Policy in March 2009 by a unanimous vote of the Senate.

He could not have been a more overt contrast to Marburger. His message on climate change (and many other policy areas with essential scientific dependencies) reached beyond the media into the Obama Administration's effort to coordinate federal efforts with research and engineering initiatives around the world. More than an ambassador for science, he was a diplomatic troubleshooter, smoothing the path for alliances with other governments and private industry. Obama got the credit; it was Holdren who moved the mountains.

And then there were the pandemics - the eruption of Ebola in West Africa in 2014, which threatened the US when a man in Dallas, having traveled to the US from Africa, was found to have the virus. He died. Ten additional cases emerged; all but one recovered.

Ebola was more scare than reality in the US, but that didn't stop Holdren; he went on PBS, describing high-tech measures to treat while containing; he met with private-sector scientists, preparing for the worst; and he led a task force created by executive order to combat antibiotic-resistant bacteria.

Five years earlier, a new virus – H1N1 – had appeared in the US, prompting Obama to declare a national emergency. More than 12,000 Americans died of the virus, but federal response was swift and effective; a vaccine was successfully deployed, and the crisis was ended by April 2010. Holdren's role? To lead an effort to overall the vaccine distribution process to get to more people more quickly, an effort he openly presented to the media, to reassure the public.

Ah, the good old days...

Anthony Fauci in the Hot Seat

We have, then, two extremes: the expert voice in the White House that tells it straight and won't back down, and the expert voice that dissembles and prevaricates for political gain.

But back in the Bartlet West Wing, it's the expert telling it straight and the administration itself dissembling and prevaricating for political gain. In the end, however, Bartlet doesn't disappoint. Griffith does offer her resignation, and they summarize the problem:

"On thinking about it, I felt your firing me would send a dangerous signal to whomever had my job next," she explains. □

"Did you not think that playing down the dangers of drug use sent a dangerous signal as well?" he asks.

"I do not believe that is what I did, sir," she replies, and of course she's correct; she's grounding the debate back in the reality of the words actually spoken, defusing the political trimmings: "I was asked, by and large, if marijuana holds the same addictive properties as heroin or LSD; it does not. I was asked if marijuana poses a greater health risk than nicotine and alcohol, and in my opinion, it does not."

And that brings us to another high-profile healthcare professional speaking truth to power, who in 2020 was faced with Griffith's dilemma: Dr. Anthony Fauci, Director of the National Institute of Allergy and Infectious Diseases, an honest and effective scientist and administrator who served six administrations, having taken his post in 1984.

At age 79, Fauci faced the challenge of a lifetime for a professional of his particular specialty: the coronavirus and the global eruption of the COVID-19 pandemic. That it happened while Fauci was the top-ranking epidemiologist in the US was certainly fortunate; that it happened on Donald Trump's watch most certainly wasn't. Fauci could not have been more equal to the task; Trump couldn't have been less so.

Fauci, who had been at Barack Obama's side through several pandemics had, in fact, predicted the coronavirus or something like it on the Trump watch: in January 2017, during an address to the Center for Global Health Science and Security at the Georgetown University Medical Center – 10 days before Trump's inauguration – he said the following:

"If there's one message that I want to leave with you today, based on my experience... there is no question that there will be a challenge to the coming administration in the arena of infectious diseases - both chronic infectious diseases, in the sense of already-ongoing disease, and we have certainly a large burden of that, but also there will be a surprise outbreak... History, and the history of the past 32 years that I've been the director of NIAID, will tell the next administration that there's no doubt in anyone's mind that they will be faced with the challenges that their predecessors were faced with." The title of the panel: "Pandemic Preparedness in the Next Administration."

And when Fauci's prediction came true in January 2020, it was he who stepped to the presidential podium to begin informing the public about the coronavirus; it was he who explained what it was and what it meant; it was he who outlined the steps necessary to limit the spread of the virus; it was he who offered up reasonable, fact-based predictions about what would happen next.

His narrative didn't come close to matching Trump's. In the early weeks of the pandemic, he careened wildly from one fictional statement to another: the virus was a hoax; the virus was a Democratic scheme to thwart his re-election; the virus was a vengeful Chinese attack on the US.

When the existence of the virus could no longer be denied and Americans were dying, his rhetoric shifted, but its unstable dynamic remained: the virus would just magically disappear before summer; it could be cleared up by injections of disinfectant; bright light shining inside the body would do the trick; and there's this hydroxychloroquine stuff...

And running parallel to Trump's snake oil pitches were his reports on his administration's success in coping with the pandemic. As the US rocketed to the front of the international pack in cases and deaths, he steadily reassured the public that he was doing an "outstanding" job of containing COVID, repeatedly insisting that if there was less testing, there would be fewer cases.

A disconnect of this magnitude between President and Expert was unprecedented. Fauci and Trump could not have offered more radically disparate accounts of the nation's reality.

It went far beyond Leo censoring the EPA, or Josh prioritizing a White House official position over medical truth, or CJ speaking for herself and not the White House; those exemplars of executive disconnect pale beside the Fauci-Trump collision. But they are connected, and in-kind, on a deeper level: they all speak to the confusion such disagreement generates in the public, on the question of who to trust. And when the coronavirus came to town, that trust was already all over the map, in the mind of the American public. As of Summer 2020, Newsweek was reporting that "a majority of Republicans say they don't trust Dr. Anthony Fauci or the Centers for Disease Control and Prevention (CDC) for advice on the coronavirus, but almost 70 percent say they trust President Donald Trump for advice... 52 percent of Republicans said they don't trust what the CDC has said about the novel virus, and 53 percent said they don't trust Fauci," according to a poll it took.

By contrast, *Newsweek*'s poll revealed that among Democrats, "a large majority said they don't trust Trump for advice on the virus but do trust Fauci and the CDC. According to the poll, 93 percent of Democrats said they don't trust the president, while 78 percent said they trust Fauci and 76 percent said they trust the CDC."

With partisan affiliation removed from the data, the results indicated that "among all respondents, 31 percent said they trust Trump for advice on the virus, 51 percent said they trust Fauci, and 55 percent said they trust the CDC. By comparison, 58 percent said they don't trust what Trump has said about the virus, 29 percent said they don't trust Fauci, and 32 percent said they don't trust the CDC."

That kind of divide is unconscionable, certainly; but the numbers lay out in stark, disheartening transparency just how messed up the collective mind of the American citizen has become, when it comes to trusting experts – and more alarming, how off-the-charts its misplaced devotion to an Authoritarian leader can be.

Per Fauci, the US is "still knee-deep in the first wave" of the pandemic; per Trump, "I think we are in a good place."

Fauci dared not openly criticize the president, lest he be dismissed (and he sorely needed to remain where he was, for the good of the nation). Trump, predictably, had no compunctions about criticizing Fauci, speaking openly to the media about the NIAID director's "mistakes."

And even that wasn't the worst of it; for daring to continue putting data ahead of Authoritarian bloviation, Fauci revealed in early August that he and his family had been getting death threats, and that he had been forced to arrange private security to protect them.

"I wouldn't have imagined in my wildest dreams that people who object to things that are pure public health principles are so set against it and don't like what you and I say, namely in the world of science, that they actually threaten you," he said.

That's how far we've wandered from the truth.

"A sluggish response by a government denuded of expertise allowed the coronavirus to gain a foothold," summarized Ed Yong in *The Atlantic*. "Chronic underfunding of public health neutered the nation's ability to prevent the pathogen's spread. A bloated, inefficient health-care system left hospitals ill-prepared for the ensuing wave of sickness. Racist policies that have endured since the days of colonization and slavery left Indigenous and Black Americans especially vulnerable to COVID-19. The decades-long process of shredding the nation's social safety net forced millions of essential workers in low-paying jobs to risk their life for their livelihood. The same social media platforms that sowed partisanship and misinformation during the 2014 Ebola outbreak in Africa and the 2016 US election became vectors for conspiracy theories during the 2020 pandemic."

"Openness is the Basis of a Free Society"

Sometimes President Bartlet got it right, of course, as when a fire in a national forest sparks controversy over the federal government's responsibility to fight it. Public sensibility (and an anxious governor) favor the federal government putting the fire out; but his environmental science advisers tell him not to:

"It's the end of the season and the fire isn't anywhere near tourists," he tells Leo." Letting this fire burn is good for the environment. You know how I know?"

"How?"

"Because smart people told me. Please, god, Leo, let them be right..."

And Sam weighs in on professional expertise, peaking not only for progressive politicians everywhere but the majority of the electorate. He's arguing with film producer Morgan Ross about the impact of TV violence on children.

"There's been a 28% drop in juvenile crime in the last five years, 10% drop in the overall crime rate," Ross tells Sam.

"I don't care," Sam replies.

"Why?"

"Because the American Academy of Pediatrics, the AMA and the American Psychological Association all say that watching violence on TV is bad for kids," Sam explains, "and we're gonna listen to the experts..."[14]

But the last word on this subject will go to Ellie, who found herself mired in White House controversy once again in "Eppur Si Muove", when a partisan attack on Bartlet was opportunistically based on her working as a research assistant for a controversial cervical cancer study that included sex workers as subjects. Bartlet is less harsh with his daughter this time around, as she obviously just wants to be left alone to do her work, but her father convinces her that science can't extricate itself from public controversy - there are times when she and those like her must take a stand.

This she does, behind the briefing room podium, giving this statement:

"While money spent studying the brains of PCP users might seem to be taxpayer waste, this research led directly to the discovery of the NMDA receptor. Science cannot exist in a vacuum. By nature, it's an open enterprise, strengthened by public scrutiny. Openness is the basis of a free society. But when science is attacked on ideological grounds, its integrity and usefulness are threatened. Independent peer-reviewed research is the cornerstone of science in America. It shouldn't be about the left or the right, but what works to keep people safe and healthy. I believe all Americans, and all people everywhere, no matter who they are or how they live, deserve research to improve their lives. Thomas Jefferson said, 'We must not be afraid to follow the truth, wherever it may lead.' Scientific truth ennobles us. It tells us who we are, where we've been, and where we're going. I believe the truth will only be found when all scientists are free to pursue it."

---

[14] In "Ellie", S2/E15.

"Everybody wakes up alive in the morning and saves a little face."

Embrace and Promote Civility

Tabitha Fortis is about to be the next US Poet Laureate, but the White House ceremony honoring her as such is waylaid by her declaration that she wants the US to sign the treaty that will remove the land mines on the 38th parallel in Asia — otherwise she'll make a big fuss.[15]

"If you voice your disagreement at a party in your honor hosted by the President with the press in attendance," Toby tells her, "then it's a gigantic deal which travels the 63 feet right to this office."

Back and forth they go, and in the end, they find middle ground.

"I was thinking, maybe... I don't know if you could do this, but I was thinking if I could get a few minutes alone with the President, so that I could tell him what I saw in Banja Luka?"

"Yeah," Toby nods, "We can do that."

---

[15] In "The US Poet Laureate", S3/E16.

On a more international scale, China is threatening North Korea over its plan to hold free elections, and the brinkmanship is escalating. The Bartlet Administration brokers a deal that averts the escalation. In Sam's office, the President gives Sam the opportunity to guess what the deal is before telling him the details:

"China agrees to stand down the war games," Sam begins.

"Right."

"And they agree to let Taiwan test the Patriots. One Patriot."

"Yes."

"And we... Please, I want to be right about this. We agree not to sell Taiwan the Aegis Destroyers for a period of... I don't know... five years?"

"Ten years, but you've got it."

"Sir, the Aegis... the Aegis radar technology isn't something that... I mean, what if Taiwan *did* fall to China? Now they have them, plus these ships cost something like $800 million apiece? Buying four of them would eat half of Taiwan's defense budget."

"And so..."

And light dawns. Sam gets that the President was bluffing all along, to calm everything down and restore civility between the Asian nations.

"You never were going to sell them the destroyers!"

The President shakes his head. "But everybody wakes up alive in the morning and saves a little face.[16]

---

[16] In "Hartsfield's Landing", S3/E14.

"Civility and being civil to others are essential to the workings of democracy. Civility is closely aligned with manners. With respect. With courtesy. With politeness," wrote Richard Haass. "To learn how to disagree without being disagreeable. To paraphrase the Golden Rule, civility is about treating others as you would like others to treat you.

"At least two former presidents have weighed in on the word," he continued. "John F. Kennedy, in his famous 'Ask not what your country can do for you - ask what you can do for your country' inaugural address, noted that 'civility is not a sign of weakness.' Forty years later, in his first inaugural address, George W. Bush expressed it this way: 'Civility is not a tactic or a sentiment; it is the determined choice of trust over cynicism, of community over chaos.' Why is this concept so important? Disagreements are inevitable in a democracy. Opinions often are strong or even emotional. The subject can be anything, be it public spending, taxes, race, gender, political and personal rights, abortion, guns, masks, vaccinations, arrangements for voting or the counting of ballots, or matters of war and peace. What civility does is make it possible for differences to be reduced or even bridged - and even if not, civility allows for dialogue and relationships to continue on other issues where agreement might not be out of the question. Opponents on one issue need not become opponents on all issues, much less enemies. Civility greatly decreases the chances that disagreements will spill over into violence. How can civility be promoted? It is best to deal with issues and arguments on their merits, not on motives you might ascribe to those making the arguments."

Our *West Wing* heroes model that strength and character in the face of adversity through their commitment to civility. The strength and character derive from the willingness to remain committed to civility even at great personal cost – prioritizing humanity-affirming traits that strengthen us all over self-interest, even self-defense.

"Andy? You're doing that thing with your face!"

On the Importance of Reading People

Here, we borrow from Sorkin's *The American President*, the prototype for *The West Wing*. Annette Bening's character, Sydney Ellen Wade, has begun a relationship with Michael Douglas's President Andrew Shepherd. He is about to break his word to her concerning support of an environmental bill for which she's lobbying, in favor of his own gun control legislation. As a lobbyist, she is adept at reading people – and has learned to read him, probably better than he'd like.

Paying close attention to body language, making eye contact, indulging in small talk might seem awfully innocuous in the context of how to push back against Authoritarianism. How could a focus on polite but irrelevant conversation possibly be a tool for resisting autocrats?

At face value, we might see some value in the undeniable positivity of human connection, however inconsequential; and we can grant that even a triviality like small talk can serve as an indicator of societal health.

Interconnectedness that defines us as human beings. And that interconnectedness makes small talk an important practice, when pushing back against the encroachment of Authoritarianism in a society. Historian Timothy Snyder, in his treatise on tyranny, recommends small talk and eye contact as important habits the freedom fighter should employ.

"This is not just polite," he wrote. "It is part of being a citizen and a responsible member of society."

In this we can infer the value he is reminding us to find in our participation in that society. Human contact needs to remain a constant in times of distressing change.

But there's more going on in what Snyder is recommending:

"It is also a way," he continued, "to stay in touch with your surroundings, break down social barriers, and understand whom you should and should not trust."

That's powerful. The idea is, *Know the people around you – for better and worse.*

That's a little discouraging, that it might be as important to use superficial social politeness as a means of scrutinizing our fellow human beings as it is to use it to brighten our days. But the pragmatism of his suggestion is undeniable, as he finally points out,

"If we enter a culture of denunciation, you will want to know the psychological landscape of your daily life."

Sobering. But crucial, all the same.

"You're my guys. And I'm yours. And there's nothing I wouldn't do for you."

Cultivate Community

Concerned about a leak to the press that might embarrass the White House, Toby gathers the communications staff together in the mess – and after making clear his displeasure, he inadvertently reveals how he feels about them all:

"We're a group. We're a team. From the President and Leo on through, we're a team...We win together, we lose together, we celebrate and we mourn together. And defeats are softened and victories sweetened because we did them together...

"I'm not gonna take anyone's head off. I'm simply gonna say this: you're my guys. And I'm yours. And there's nothing I wouldn't do for you."[17]

Bearing the distinction of being the only Republican in the Bartlet Administration, excepting Assistant Secretary of State Albie Duncan, Ainsley Hayes has found serving in the White

---

[17] In "War Crimes", S3/E5.

House Counsel's office a challenging experience. But she soldiers on, determined to live up to the honor of being called to serve – and the senior staff get over their partisan discomfort and welcome her fully, celebrating her in her own office as Gilbert & Sullivan plays in the background.

Toby's appreciation of his staff as a community and President Bartlet's inner circle welcoming Ainsley as one of their own are both expressions of both the power of and importance of community. Community means mutual support; community means shared values. Community means strong and meaningful bonds. All of which threaten the Authoritarian.

The Authoritarian seeks to divide. By parsing populations into "Loyal" and "Other" and providing each with different rhetoric, he keeps people from seeing for themselves the machinations at work, rearranging their lives to suit his purposes.

Among people living in true community, those kinds of machinations don't remain hidden. When people who live side by side every day reconcile their differing worldviews and refuse to let them distract from their understanding of those they are living alongside, the Authoritarian's deceits can't take root.

"We all live in a context, in a society," wrote Richard Haass. "We have a stake in the overall well-being of that society, which in turn translates into our having a stake in the well-being of our fellow citizens. As poet and priest John Donne wrote, 'No man is an island entire of itself; every man is a piece of the continent, a part of the main.'

"There are both moral and practical reasons for caring about our fellow Americans. The former is simply caring for others for their sake. The question is a familiar one: Am I my brother's or sister's keeper? To some extent we should be and need to be. This teaching can be found in many of the world's major religions. The New Testament instructs, 'Look not every man on his own things, but every man also on the things of others.' In Judaism, the notion is captured by the theme that 'all of Israel are responsible for one another.' Various Hindu texts contain verses that elaborate on the theme of the world as one family, calling on individuals to treat others equally and as they would want to be treated. This sense of obligation to one's fellow man or woman is the basis of a great deal of volunteerism and charity. At best this is an argument for choosing to do good things that assist others; at a minimum, it is an argument for avoiding doing things that injure others.

"There is another reason for caring about others," he continued. "Doing so reflects our self-interest and is for our own sake. Martin Luther King Jr. made such an argument in his 'Letter from a Birmingham Jail': 'We are caught in an inescapable network of mutuality, tied in a single garment of destiny. Whatever affects one directly affects all indirectly.' In many ways the trajectories of other people's lives intersect with our own and the consequences can be significant and, unfortunately, not always beneficial. Strangers and neighbors alike can be sources of contagion by carrying infectious disease or a burden on public health stemming from abuse of drugs or alcohol. People can turn to crime for a host of reasons and even if there is no intent can act irresponsibly with guns or cars. Then there is the reality that there are those who do not contribute what they could to society and the economy and as a result increase the financial burden of the rest of us. All this adds up to a strong case that the obligation to care for others, be it for their sake or our own, is critical for a democratic society. Teddy Roosevelt, in his inaugural address more than a century ago, posited that 'our relations with the other powers of the world are important, but still more important are our relations among ourselves.'"

Robert Putnam commented on how isolation and loneliness are perilous to democracy, in a *New York Times* interview:

"What we've seen over the last 25 years is a deepening and intensifying of that trend. We've become more socially isolated, and we can see it in every facet in our lives. We can see it in the surgeon general's talk about loneliness. He's been talking recently about the psychological state of being lonely. Social isolation leads to lots of bad things. It's bad for your health, but it's *really* bad for the country, because people who are isolated, and especially young men who are isolated, are vulnerable to the appeals of some false community. I can cite chapter and verse on this: Eager recruits to the Nazi Party in the 1930s were lonely young German men, and it's not an accident that the people who are attracted today to white nationalist groups are lonely young white men. Loneliness: it's bad for your health, but it's also bad for the health of the people around you."

He explores the impact of isolation and loneliness on Americans without community in *Bowling Alone:*

"Without a strong sense of social belonging, individuals are more prone to loneliness and isolation," he wrote. "A sense of belonging is fundamental to human well-being."

And

"In a world of increasing individualism, we must find ways to rebuild the social ties that once held us together."

And

"The more connected we are to our communities, the happier and healthier we tend to be."

And, most tellingly,

"Civic participation is not just a privilege, but a responsibility of every citizen."

And

"People divorced from community, occupation, and association are first and foremost among the supporters of extremism." All the more reason to get to work on cultivating community!

The Bartlet Administration includes a great many people, from lots of different places and backgrounds, united into one community to form a cooperative for the purposes of mutual care and support.

In opposing the Authoritarian, the cultivation of this sort of community with those unlike ourselves is one of the surest deterrents of the Authoritarian's threat.

"So, tell me, how can I be of service to you? If it's within my power to give, you shall have it!"

Make International Friends

Lord John Marbury – women love him, men want to have a drink with him. Unless they're Leo.

England's Ambassador to the United States appears frequently, always ready to assist President Bartlet and his team when international tensions arise.

"The world is coming apart at the seams," the President says on the first such occasion.

"Well, then," Lord Marbury replies, "Thank God you sent for me!"[18]

Lord John Marbury is just one of many international allies of the Bartlet Administration – friends abroad, from different nations and cultures, sharing our values and priorities and vision for the future of the world. Fighting for the same things.

We've already heard from Mark Twain, above, on the power

---

[18] In "Lord John Marbury", S1/E11.

of international experience to diminish our prejudices and open us to diversity. But Timothy Snyder clues us in on another benefit to international friendships: they serve to strengthen us against the Authoritarian, by expanding our knowledge base about and resources with which to oppose growing tyranny.

"Learn from peers in other countries," he advised. Our European friends, after all, have a lot more experience with autocrats and tyrants than we do.

It's also advantageous, he points out, to have safe harbors beyond our own borders:

"Keep up your friendships abroad, or make new friends in other countries. The present difficulties in the United States are an element of a larger trend. And no country is going to find a solution by itself. Make sure you and your family have passports.

"The fact that most Americans do not have passports has become a problem for American democracy. Sometimes Americans say that they do not need travel documents, because they prefer to die defending freedom in America. These are fine words, but they miss an important point. The fight will be a long one. Even if it does require sacrifice, it first demands sustained attention to the world around us, so that we know what we are resisting, and how best to do so. So having a passport is not a sign of surrender. On the contrary, it is liberating, since it creates the possibility of new experiences. It allows us to see how other people, sometimes wiser than we, react to similar problems. Since so much of what is happening now is familiar to the rest of the world or from recent history, we must observe and listen."

The rising Authoritarianism in the US is being echoed even now in Europe, and the truth is, we're all in it together – Americans, Hungarians, Ukrainians, Poles. In opposing it, we must be united; like the US and its parent nation England, we're simply stronger together.

And we get together by doing just that – getting together.

"You'll denounce these people, Al. You'll do it publicly. And until you do, you can all get your fat asses out of my White House!"

Renounce Violence

President Bartlet is furious that an extreme religious group has made a violent gesture toward his granddaughter, and wants Al Caldwell's own religious organization to distance itself from those who would do violence to advance their cause.[19]

This action point needs little embellishment. To oppose the violence of the Authoritarian with counter-violence is to invoke Friedrich Nietzsche: "When you fight the dragon, beware, lest you become a dragon!"

Haass has some very specific advice on this point:

"What makes a democracy different from authoritarian systems is that democracy offers peaceful channels for individuals and groups to pursue their political and economic

---

[19] In "Pilot", S1/E1.

policy aims," Haass wrote. "They do so without any guarantee that they will achieve their goals, but they accept the legitimacy of the process, as they believe they will have a fair chance of succeeding in part or in whole over time. They also believe that no particular issue merits undermining the value of the political system as a whole.

"Nevertheless, the temptation arises from time to time for some to pursue political goals with physical force. It can stem from conviction, that a goal is so worthy that the ends justify the means, or from frustration, that there is no other available path to take to achieve one's goals and that the goals are judged to be so important they must be met no matter the price.

"frustration, that there is no other available path to take to achieve one's goals and that the goals are judged to be so important they must be met no matter the price."

Haass goes on to cite the commitment of Martin Luther King, Jr. and Mahatma Gandhi to nonviolent protest as the better way. Finally, he concludes,

"The need to minimize political violence also requires that a premium be placed on making the political and legal system fair and responsive, that there be a level playing field. This holds especially true for those entrusted with special power, such as the police. Acceptance of the legitimacy of the state and its monopoly on the use of force is predicated on its willingness to exercise restraint, to use force lawfully, and to hold anyone who is an officer of the state accountable. This is necessary to reduce the chance that American democracy will fall victim to widespread violence."

"They're gonna throw rocks at you next week, and I wanted to be standing next to you when they did."

Let Others Know, 'You Are Not Alone!'

When Josh's PTSD from being shot at Rosslyn boils over and Leo calls in a therapist from the American Trauma Victims Association, Josh emerges from the session to find both Leo and Donna waiting for him.[20]

"This guy's walking down a street, when he falls in a hole. The walls are so steep. He can't get out. A doctor passes by, and the guy shouts up 'Hey you! Can you help me out?' The doctor writes him a prescription, throws it down the hole and moves on. Then a priest comes along and the guy shouts up 'Father, I'm down in this hole, can you help me out?' The priest writes out a prayer, throws it down in the hole and moves on. Then a friend walks by. 'Hey Joe, it's me, can you help me out?' And the friend jumps in the hole! Our guy says, 'Are you stupid? Now we're both down here!' and the friend

---

[20] In "Noël", S2/E10.

says, 'Yeah, but I've been down here before, and I know the way out!'

"As long as I got a job, you got a job, you understand?"

Because he made a promise to a widow, Sam is running for Congress in the California 47th. But it's a bright red district and he has no chance. In the final days of his campaign, Toby and Josh come on board to point him back in the direction of his true values and convictions.[21]

"There's no chance of a miracle?" Sam asks Toby.

"No."

"You're gonna lose, and you're gonna lose huge," Toby tells him honestly. "They're gonna throw rocks at you next week, and I wanted to be standing next to you when they did."

Sometimes there's nothing lonelier than trying to fight for your beliefs in isolation. Trying to go it alone can be devastatingly painful and difficult. When Leo and Donna assure Josh they're right there with him, his burden is lightened; when Sam faces his California struggle, Toby assures him they will face it together.

Isolation and loneliness are tough enough to endure in themselves. Human beings are social creatures, through and through; we are not meant to be alone.

But isolation and loneliness are tougher still when accompanied by hopelessness and despair – and that is exactly the burden the Authoritarian heaps on those he would put down and repress. The isolation and despair are intended to extinguish hope – and, thereby, opposition.

---

[21] In "Red Haven's on Fire", S4/E17.

"In all struggles... strugglers, fighters, resistors or peasant/organic intellectuals have tended to start and sustain the struggles either alone or with very few comrades in arms," wrote Yusuf Serunkuma in *Review of the African Political Economy*. "Because these moments tend to be long and winding, they come with corrosive spells of loneliness - and are often exhausting. The toll could be either mental or material or both."

Serunkuma commented on "a deeply personal, emotional and introspective piece" by alejandra ciriza, in which she "recollects the memories of struggle and exile after the 1976 coup in her home country of Argentina which brought in the murderous government of the *Cono Sur*. ciriza writes that the military junta that headed the coup in 1976 was so brutal that political persecution by the state included, 'systematic use of terror, in broad daylight, forced disappearance, murder, confinement, and censorship, but [also] the methodical inculcation of fear'. Reflecting on this condition, as one of those who had been active in resisting the junta, ciriza recalls the pains of exile, the pain of brutal defeat, and hopelessness about the future: 'It was a harsh isolation. The absences transformed into permanent anguish, the endless searches in the newspapers looking for a name ... among the fallen'.

"'So, this is what largely defeat is all about,' she writes, capturing the pain of loneliness when friends and comrades have been exiled or murdered. 'The isolation, the rupture of the threads of collective fabric, of the connections with others, so indispensable for us to think and struggle, of loss of emancipatory horizons, which can be envisioned when the masses become conscious of their powers'. These different reflections on loneliness provide a spectrum of reflections covering different modes of struggle."

ciriza was writing in circumstances far harsher than most in the US have ever known, but the dynamic captured is the same: the Authoritarian's isolation and disruption do more than sever connection between allies; they generate an immobilizing anguish and pain. It is the duty, then, of those resisting the Authoritarian to respond to that.

When we hear a lonely and isolated voice out there on our landscape, losing hope as the clouds gather, we need to answer.

"Damned if 28 US Senators haven't just walked onto the floor to help."

Have a Support System

Senator Howard Stackhouse stands alone, rambling on about recipes and card game rules to an empty Senate chamber. He's eight hours on in filibustering to stall a vote on a family healthcare bill, one that he desperately wants to include money for child autism treatment and education.[22]

When, thanks to Donna, the staff figures out what he's up to, they move heaven and earth to help him. CJ tells her father about it in an email:

"Tonight, I've seen a man with no legs stay standing, Dad, and a guy with no voice keep shouting - and if politics brings out the worst in people, then maybe people bring out the best — 'cause I'm looking at the TV right now, and damned if 28 US Senators haven't just walked onto the floor to help."

CJ's father Tal is suffering from dementia and rapidly declining — and when she visits to see how he's doing, he

---

[22] In "The Stackhouse Filibuster", S2/E17.

learns that her stepmother Molly has abandoned him, leading to a confrontation.[23]

"Do you know what the nickname for the disease is?" her stepmother asks. "'The Long Goodbye'."

"Well, not in your case, though, is it?" CJ angrily replies. "In your case, more accurately it's the short "see you later goodbye', isn't it'

"What happened to reciprocity? Do you ever imagine in a million years if the roles were reversed he would ever do this to you? This is - what you're doing right now - invalidates everything that came before all the good, the years of teaching. This cancels a good and valuable life. He needs you!"

We have seen, above, several examples of the first – cultivating community, pushing back against isolation and loneliness, promoting civility, embracing diversity, being mindful of focused human contact, breaching cultural barriers – all of these provide strength to us and those we work with, as well as a vast array of supporting emotional resources.

And we know that investigation, advocacy for truth, giving to causes that matter, improving our use of language, proactivity, practicing civil disobedience, defending our institutions, and enforcing privacy all serve our mission.

We need to build up groups around us of people who will support us in these ways – and whom we can support in turn. An individual fighting the Authoritarian is easily dispatched; a committed group of allies, not so much. There are no White House senior staffs of one.

We need to seek out the CJs and Mollies and Donnas who will stand strong with us, building that strength through

---

[23] In "The Long Goodbye", S4/E13.

community and human contact; defending dignity through civility and inclusion, pushing through cultural divides – those who will bond with us as we do the work – showing up, investigating, defending those things that need defending, speaking the truth, speaking out against bad laws, rising up in peaceful protest.

The convenient aspect of this support system building is that it happens through exactly these actions.

Educating yourself about issues at the local level will inform you about who stands where on those issues. You can see who needs your support. Cultivating community brings you into contact with those who have something to offer you and to whom you in turn can offer support. Across cultural and geographic divides, you'll find more allies still, diverse ones with fresh viewpoints and backgrounds that will inform you. And the sharpening skill of eye contact and enhanced attention in personal interaction will help you sense who you can trust and who you can't.

As these relationships develop, you can enter into privacy agreements with your companions, reinforcing good personal data hygiene. The same applies to mindfulness of language – both the dog whistles of the Authoritarian and his followers, and your own renewed ability to frame. Discuss that framing, and those dog whistles, with your team.

Like most aspects of resistance, this one will vary a great deal, person to person. Your support system will be just that – yours. Unlike any others. The trick is to do a better job of it than Howard Stackhouse or Tal Cregg did; don't convince yourself you can do it all on your own. Find your Molly! Find your 28 Senators!

"We must not be afraid to follow the truth wherever it may lead."

Affirm Truth, Wherever You Find It

Back in law school, Sam studied the case of Daniel Galt, a state department employee who was accused of colluding with the Kremlin. The paper he wrote finds its way to Donna's old college roommate, Galt's granddaughter, who asks Sam to look into the possibility of a pardon for her grandfather – a symbolic gesture only, as he's long dead. She turns to Sam because his paper, she believes, demonstrated his innocence.[24]

National Security Advisor Nancy McNally intervenes to wave Sam off; not only was Galt guilty of espionage, he was a valuable Russian asset codenamed Blackwater.

Faced with this new evidence, Sam not only abandons his previous belief, he embraces the truth about Galt to the degree that he is emotionally agitated; Galt's guilt offends him. He doesn't rationalize his mistake; he commits to the facts.

---

[24] In "Somebody's Going to Emergency, Somebody's Going to Jail", S2/E16.

Ellie Bartlet, targeted by partisan provocateurs in a squabble of research appropriations, is challenged by her father to speak out: partisans have been corrosive to truth and fact for centuries, and voices like hers must be raised to stand against them, he tells her.[25]

She holds a press conference and follows through:

"Openness is the basis of a free society. But when science is attacked on ideological grounds, its integrity and usefulness are threatened," she says to the roomful of reporters. "I believe all Americans and all people everywhere, no matter who they are or how they live, deserve research to improve their lives. Thomas Jefferson said, 'We must not be afraid to follow the truth wherever it may lead.'"

Seeking out truth, standing on truth, is a cornerstone of resistance of Authoritarianism.

"To abandon facts is to abandon freedom," wrote Snyder. "If nothing is true, then no one can criticize power, because there is no basis upon which to do so. If nothing is true, then all is spectacle. The biggest wallet pays for the most blinding lights.

"You submit to tyranny when you renounce the difference between what you want to hear and what is actually the case," he continued. "This renunciation of reality can feel natural and pleasant, but the result is your demise as an individual—and thus the collapse of any political system that depends upon individualism."

And it's not just that letting go of fact strengthens tyranny as it weakens liberty; it's that the embrace of truth, across the spectrum of life, fortifies that life.

"Fascists despised the small truths of daily existence, loved

---

slogans that resonated like a new religion, and preferred creative myths to history or journalism," he wrote. "They used new media, which at the time was radio, to create a drumbeat of propaganda that aroused feelings before people had time to ascertain facts. And now, as then, many people confused faith in a hugely flawed leader with the truth about the world we all share. Post-truth is pre-fascism."

Mycielski offers some specifics here, articulating how the Authoritarian will make his assault on truth:

- "They will subjugate state media, turning them into a propaganda tube. Then, through convoluted laws and threats they will attempt to control all mainstream media and limit press freedom. They will ban critical press from their briefings, calling them 'liars', 'fake news'. They will brand those media as "unpatriotic", acting against the People. *Fight for every media outlet, every journalist that is being banned, censored, sacked or labelled an "enemy of the state" – there's no hope for freedom where there is no free press.*
- "They will distort the truth, deny facts and blatantly lie. They will try to make you forget what facts are, sedate your need to find the truth. They will feed "post-truths" and "alternative facts", replace knowledge and logic with emotions and fiction. *Always think critically, fact-check and point out the truth, expose ignorance with facts.*
- "They will incite and then leak fake, superficial "scandals". They will smear opposition with trivial accusations, blowing them out of proportion and then feeding the flame. This is just smokescreen for the legal steps they will be taking towards totalitarianism. *See through superficial topics in mainstream media and focus on what they are actually doing.*"

85

The phrase "Affirm truth, wherever you find it" is not actually from either Snyder or Mycielski; it's a quote from Rob Bell, an Evangelical pastor – who breaks with his peers in believing that embracing truth is essential for its own sake – even if that truth flies in the face of doctrine and dogma. The message is all the more powerful, given the messenger.

Once you've reached the truth – stand firm on it.

"Simon was a Big Brother to a kid named Anthony Marcus..."

Get in the Habit of Giving

Special Agent Simon Donovan, assigned to protect CJ Cregg when she starts receiving death threats, shows up at the White House unexpectedly while off duty with a black teenager named Anthony, for whom he has the greatest affection. CJ and Carol are surprised.[26]

"I'm a Big Brother," Simon explains to CJ later. "We've been together about three years."

"Are you good at it?"

"I don't know. He says he wants to be a Big Brother when he gets older, so I guess..."

"No one has ever become poor by giving," said Anne Frank, and she is in good company. "I have found that among its other benefits, giving liberates the soul of the giver," said Maya Angelou.

And, from Confucius, "He who wishes to secure the good of

---

[26] In "Posse Comitatus", S3/E21.

others has already secured his own."

The act of giving promotes social health in a way that pushes back against those who would corrupt it, according to Timothy Snyder:

"Contribute to good causes," he wrote. "Be active in organizations, political or not, that express your own view of life. Pick a charity or two and set up autopay. Then you will have made a free choice that supports civil society and helps others to do good.

"When Americans think of freedom, we usually imagine a contest between a lone individual and a powerful government. We tend to conclude that the individual should be empowered and the government kept at bay. This is all well and good. But one element of freedom is the choice of associates, and one defense of freedom is the activity of groups to sustain their members. This is why we should engage in activities that are of interest to us, our friends, our families. These need not be expressly political: Václav Havel, the Czech dissident thinker, gave the example of brewing good beer.

"Insofar as we take pride in these activities, and come to know others who do so as well, we are creating civil society. Sharing in an undertaking teaches us that we can trust people beyond a narrow circle of friends and families, and helps us to recognize authorities from whom we can learn. The capacity for trust and learning can make life seem less chaotic and mysterious, and democratic politics more plausible and attractive."

We can't all donate to every cause we believe in. But there are more ways to give, and more who need what we can offer, than we can possibly count – as Simon Donovan's giving of his time to Anthony demonstrates. It strengthens us, the giver, and it strengthens the receiver – as it weakens the Authoritarian.

"Leo, if I wasn't working here, I'd probably be with them down there!"

Don't Rule Out Civil Disobedience

It's Big Block of Cheese Day, and Toby is late to the assignments meeting because he was "waylaid" by protesters. The protesters do not impress him.[27]

"In my day, we knew how to protest," he tells the room.

"What day was that?" CJ asks.

"1968."

"How the hell old were you when you were protesting?"

"My sisters took me."

On a more serious note, Josh's friend Billy Molina stages a protest of his own, along with others, camping in a live target range and preventing Navy ships from using the target range to acquire the combat certification they require to be deployed.[28]

---

[27] In "Somebody's Going to Emergency, Somebody's Going to Jail", S2/E16.

[28] In "The Two Bartlets", S3/E12.

Josh resents it when Leo puts him on the phone with Billy, but it all works out; the target range is cleared, in exchange for a meeting to discuss the Navy's disposal of contaminated shells in Puerto Rico and the cancer they are causing.

So important is this to Josh that he bails on a planned Tahitian vacation with Amy Gardner.

It's not clear that there was anything out of order when Toby tagged along to his sisters' protests, but Josh's friend Billy and his crowd were breaking the law when they invaded a Navy target range. We have a term for that sort of law-breaking: *civil disobedience*. Pushing back against injustice or harmful activity, often at great personal cost.

The Greek playwright Sophocles was a pacesetter in this regard, presenting in *Antigone* a title character who perfectly embodies the concept. Antigone, daughter of Oedipus, defies her father's successor Creon in insisting on a burial for her brother Polynices, declaring that the dictates of her conscience outweigh the king's decree. She ends up paying for her disobedience with her life, a price she declares not too dear.

Henry David Thoreau's treatise on the subject is an American classic:

"I was not made to be forced," he wrote in *On the Duty of Civil Disobedience*. "Let us see who is the strongest."

And this:

"Must the citizen ever for a moment, or in the least degree, resign his conscience to the legislator? Why has every man a conscience, then? I think that we should be men first, and subjects afterward. It is not desirable to cultivate a respect for the law, so much as for the right. The only obligation which I have a right to assume is to do at any time what I think right."

And this:

"A common and natural result of an undue respect of law is, that you may see a file of soldiers, colonel, captain, corporal, privates, powder-monkeys, and all, marching in admirable order over hill and dale to the wars, against their wills, ay, against their common sense and consciences, which makes it very steep marching indeed, and produces a palpitation of the heart."

And this:

""Let your life be a counter-friction to stop the machine. What I have to do is to see, at any rate, that I do not lend myself to the wrong which I condemn."

Civil disobedience can take many forms, of course. The prominent examples in American history include the Boston Tea Party, when New England colonists threw a cargo of British East India Tea into Boston Harbor, flagrantly breaking the law to protest an unjust and exploitative tax; Rosa Parks took her famous bus ride in Montgomery, Alabama, refusing to sit in the back of the bus because her skin color rendered her a second-class citizen in the eyes of her white neighbors. Around the nation, young men burned their draft cards – risking prison – to protest the Vietnam War, which the US government was forcing them to fight for dubious reasons.

An act of law-breaking, an act of rule-breaking; both acts of resistance. And there are still more:

- **Leaking sensitive information.** Leaking information that reveals covert abuses of authority, such as civil rights violations. Also known as "whistleblowing", this form of civil disobedience has often extended to pushback against corporations acting in their own interests at the expense of the public. In cases involving military and other government secrets, it might be considered espionage.
- **Demonstrations.** It is not uncommon, in the US and many other countries, for protesters to stage unregistered marches, rallies, and other demonstrations to protest what they perceive as

injustice or abuse of power. This is sometimes problematic, as the stated purpose of such registration is to provide authorities with the opportunity to ensure the safety of the protestors; all too often, in the past, such registration has been withheld, not over safety issues, but to quell protest – which is why many demonstrators will simply employ civil disobedience and protest illegally, rather than be silenced.

- **Sit-ins**. A variation on general demonstrations such as rallies and marches, sit-ins are specifically designed to obstruct traffic or access to buildings or some other inconvenience, as a means of drawing attention to an issue. The idea is to provoke a police response, usually to draw the media, and may include extremes such as handcuffing oneself to a fence or a gate. The actor Martin Sheen, who portrayed a progressive US president on *The West Wing*, prides himself on having been arrested dozens of times at sit-in demonstrations. They are illegal, and therefore attention-getting, for a reason: they carry risk, as such obstruction could potentially create a public hazard by blocking infrastructure in a way that constrains emergency vehicles and personnel.

- **Occupation.** A variation on the sit-in, this form of protest is basically a demonstration that doesn't end: protesters move into an area and just stay there, daring the law to move them. The locale can be a building, a parking lot, a bus station, a public park – any place that people aren't allowed to stay indefinitely. This, too, can result in breaking the law. The Occupy Wall Street movement, a 2011 populist movement in which tens of thousands of New York City citizens protested the 2008 bank bailouts and the 2010 US Supreme Court Citizens

United ruling, was such an occupation. It lasted 59 days.

Thoreau was, of course, exactly right: failure to stand up to Authoritarian abuses and moral offenses is, in its own way, likewise a moral offense; no one stands innocent when they ignore their own impulses of conscience.

Is this risky behavior? Of course it is, as the fictional Antigone discovered. Not everyone becomes a hero for doing the right thing, as Rosa Parks did.

Josh and his friend Billy got it right: when they're doing things they shouldn't, and people are getting hurt, you put yourself on the line.

If and when that moment comes, what will you do?

"Even Fox is treating it as a seminar on the resiliency of the Constitution!"

Defending Our Institutions

President Bartlet invokes the 25th Amendment, choosing to step down from the presidency in the aftermath of his daughter's kidnapping. Since John Hoynes is no longer vice president, Speaker of the House Glen Allen Walken is sworn in. This orderly but unusual succession causes some consternation, but it preserves the peaceful transfer of power – and is, President Bartlet realizes, the right thing for the country under the circumstances.[29]

Leaning on the Constitution as he does, Jed Bartlet is taking a courageous step to preserve a principle that is essential to the functioning of the nation's highest office. It is about standing for a fundamental institution – the kind of stance that is crucial, when the Authoritarian threatens them.

"It is institutions that help us to preserve decency," Tim Snyder wrote. "They need our help as well. Do not speak of 'our institutions' unless you make them yours by acting on their

---

[29] In "25", S4/E23.

---

behalf."

Bartlet's decision to step down via the path provided by the Constitution is more than responsible behavior; it is a reinforcement of an idea that gets all too little respect in the real world today – setting aside partisanship for the good of the country. President Bartlet's actions display the ownership and investment in our fundamental institutions that Snyder is portraying as essential to any society worth fighting for.

"Institutions do not protect themselves," Snyder added, "so choose an institution you care about and take its side."

It's important to note, in considering *The West Wing*'s take on Snyder's idea, that the institution being defended is itself utterly non-partisan – the crucible of democracy itself, self-governance. Yes, democracy must push back against autocracy – but a war of ideas is ultimately just that, a struggle between two concepts of human governance. That's not the same as war between people, who need not make war on one another just because they disagree.

It's encouraging to consider *The West Wing*'s embrace of this essential theme.

"Mothers are standing in front of tanks."

Remain Calm

A genocide is escalating in the Equatorial Republic of Kundu, a crisis the Bartlet White House has been constantly monitoring. Thanks to a nudge from Will Bailey, President Bartlet is now paying very close attention to how the Kundunese are responding to the violent, oppressive regime that has suddenly taken over their country.[30]

"You know, it's easy to watch the news and think of Kundunese as either hapless victims or crazed butchers, and it turns out that's not true," he says to the senior staff in the Oval Office. "I got this intelligence summary this afternoon. 'Mothers are standing in front of tanks.' And we're going to go get their backs."

"Be calm when the unthinkable arrives," Timothy Snyder warned. "Modern tyranny is terror management. When the terrorist attack comes, remember that Authoritarians exploit such events in order to consolidate power. The sudden disaster

---

[30] In "Inauguration: Over There", S4/E15.

that requires the end of checks and balances, the dissolution of opposition parties, the suspension of freedom of expression, the right to a fair trial, and so on, is the oldest trick in the Hitlerian book. *Do not fall for it.*"

He also noted that no less than Framer James Madison advocated active response to such terror tactics, particularly in precarious circumstances:

"James Madison nicely made the point that tyranny arises 'on some favorable emergency.' After the Reichstag fire, Hannah Arendt wrote that 'I was no longer of the opinion that one can simply be a bystander.' One coup has been attempted. A failed coup is usually practice for a successful one. The emergency might be more favorable next time, and we cannot afford to be surprised."

Mycielski pointed out that one way the Authoritarian tries to get us to lose our heads is by striking at innocents whose violation will provoke our response:

"When invading your liberal sensibilities, they will focus on what hurts the most – women and minorities," he wrote. "They will act as if democracy was majority rule without respect for the minority. They will paint foreigners and immigrants as potential threats. Racial, religious, sexual and other minorities will become enemies to the order and security they are supposedly providing. They will challenge women's social status, undermine gender equality and interfere with reproductive rights. But it means they are aware of the threat women and minorities pose to their rule, so make it your strength.

"Women and minorities have to be ready to fight the hardest – reminding the majority what true democracy is about – and you must fight together with them."

Don't be intimidated. Don't be frightened. Remain calm.

"Decisions are made by those who show up!"

Answer the Call; Take a Stand

At President Bartlet's request, Leo offers the job of Associate White House Counsel to Republican Ainsley Hayes. She is taken aback, because she is ideologically at odds the the administration. But Leo reassures her, and she answers the call.[31]

"The President likes smart people who disagree with him. He wants to hear from you. The President's asking you to serve – and everything else is crap!"

Having already rejected Josh's offer to join the Hoynes Campaign, Sam nonetheless looks at Josh's face after he has encountered Jed Bartlet – and without even thinking, he walks off the job, forfeiting a prestigious law firm partnership,

---

[31] In "In This White House", S2/E4.

to be part of something that will clearly be worth the sacrifice.[32]

"That guy gets death threats because he's black and he dates your daughter. He was warned: 'Do not show up to this place. Your life will be in danger!' He said, 'To hell with that, I'm going anyway.' *You* said No! Prudent, or not prudent, this 21-year-old at $600 a week says, 'I'm going where I want to - because a man stands up!'"[33]

Take a stand! Answer the call! That's the *West Wing* formula for getting things done. It's not enough to be competent; we have to be proactive, perhaps even aggressive.

"Someone has to," wrote Timothy Snyder. "It is easy to follow along. It can feel strange to do or say something different. But without that unease, there is no freedom. Remember Rosa Parks. The moment you set an example, the spell of the status quo is broken, and others will follow."

Richard Haass added this:

"A democracy depends on the participation of its citizens," he wrote. It is rule by the people rather than of the people. Yes, in a representative democracy elected and appointed officials wield a great deal of power, but the point is that this power is derived from those who elect them and give them the power to act. The Declaration of Independence explicitly makes this point: 'Governments are instituted among men, deriving their just powers from the consent of the governed.' This all requires, though, that citizens take an active part in their democracy. It may seem hard to believe that they would not, in that people fought and died for the American colonies to become an

---

[32] In "In the Shadow of Two Gunmen", S2/E1.

[33] In "Let Bartlet Be Bartlet", S1/E19.

independent, democratic country not subjugated to a king or to a parliament they had no influence over. But in fact many Americans do not participate actively in their democracy. It is ironic that we have gone to war for the right of others to be free but all too often seem content not to take advantage of the reality that we are."

He provided some concrete examples (also invoking Rosa Parks):

"There are many other ways to bolster democracy beyond voting and direct involvement in politics. What is more, you need not be famous or powerful to make a difference. As former Secretary of Defense James Mattis pointed out, 'The impact of participation trickles up. Rosa Parks didn't start out by taking on all of Jim Crow; she started out by taking a seat on a local bus.' A group of parents initiated what turned out to be a successful recall of three members of San Francisco's school board in 2022. One woman, after losing a family member in an automobile accident, came up with the idea that became Mothers Against Drunk Driving (MADD), an organization that over the past four decades has saved countless lives. Or take gerrymandering, the process by which the majority party in a state legislature draws the lines of congressional or state legislative districts in an attempt to disadvantage the minority party. (A second consequence of gerrymandering is to increase extremism, as districts tend to be dominated by one or the other party, thereby reducing the need for candidates to attract votes from the political center in order to build a majority.) In Michigan, the entire process was turned around by a woman with no political experience who in the wake of the 2016 election used social media to launch a volunteer movement that took the power to draw districts from the state government and awarded it to an independent commission."

And this, from Robert Putnam:

"A successful democracy requires active participation and engagement from its citizens."

Lofty goals are meaningless without the will and

determination to pursue them; you have to take chances, stand out in the crowd.

"He's not gonna stop till he drops!"

Don't Give Up!

Hot on the trail of the truth about Abdul Shareef's death, Danny Concannon doesn't have any quit in him at all; whatever the right and wrong of it, the most important consideration is the truth.[34]

Howard Stackhouse, fighting for his grandson and millions of young children like him, stands alone in the Senate chamber hour after hour, refusing to budge – nothing will stop him from getting those kids the help they need.[35]

Exactly right.

Perseverance is the most important factor in resisting the Authoritarian. All the others come to nothing if they are, in the end, abandoned.

Mycielski's essay provides a list of rules centered on perseverance:

---

[34] In "Holy Night", S4/E11.

[35] In "The Stackhouse Filibuster", S2/E17.

- **Don't stay indifferent.** "It will concern you eventually. It *will* concern your family, your friends. Voice your objection *immediately!* Resist!"
- **Expose them.** "They thrive on *fear & ignorance.* Expose their scaremongering, show flaws in their arguments. They will try to distort *facts*, rewrite history – *educate* people around you."
- **Organize, mobilize!** "They're well-organized, so should you be. *Flood the streets.* They *will* back off when they see your numbers."
- **Don't let them divide you.** "… into different classes of citizens, 'true Americans', 'patriots' vs. 'traitors', 'enemies of the state'. You're *all* citizens, *one* nation – make diversity your *strength!*"
- **Don't give up!** "Don't get tired, and don't try to wait it out. Don't hope it will pass. It *won't.*"
- **Once they're out, keep them out.** "If you don't get them to back off or to step down, you better make goddamn *sure* that when the next elections come, assuming there's still any democracy left, *no one* will vote for the same bastards again!"

That level of commitment is not just essential – it's existential. If enough people don't reach it, and stick with it, democracy is over.

And achieving that commitment requires a solid foundation of values that inspire and support it. They are values *The West Wing* modeled for us, again and again, and they are presented in the pages that follow.

KNOW WHAT WE'RE FOR

The West Wing's Call to Commitment

Commitment to Core Values

Before we can answer a call to action, we have to do a self-assessment; it's not enough to simply stand against something; we must be clear on what it is we're *for*. What we're fighting against is blatantly clear; what we're fighting *for* is not always so easily articulated.

The answer, of course, is that we're fighting for our values; we're fighting for the things we believe in. It's important, then, to define those things as precisely as we can, and to be able to articulate them to others.

In the *The West Wing* universe, those values and principles are clear: they include an opposition to tyranny, of course, but its reciprocal – egalitarianism – is embraced. Diversity and social equality are paramount; truth, the greater good, the rights of all, freedom for everyone – these all naturally follow. Ensuring that everyone has a voice, and deriving an enduring unity from acceptance of that idea, wraps it all together.

A renewed commitment to those values, expressed below in *West Wing* terms, is the starting point of meaningful action in resisting the Authoritarian.

"400,000 troops and a battery of Patriot missiles for thinking about *having an election!"*

Resisting Authoritarianism

Taiwan is considering holding free elections. China isn't happy about that. Leo discusses it with Josh:

"They need 400,000 troops on high alert for thinking about holding an election. 400,000 troops and a battery of Patriot missiles for *thinking about* having an election!"[36]

President Nimbala of the Equatorial Republic of Kundu is in the White House, working with Toby and pharmaceutical executives to arrange lower prices for much-needed medicine for his country. President Bartlet calls him into the Oval Office to inform him that his country's military has taken over in his absence.[37]

"Mr. President, three hours ago there was a coup in your

---

[36] In "Hartsfield's Landing", S3/E14.

[37] In "In This White House", S2/E4.

country. The AFRC has taken the capital. They have the capital, they have the radio station, they have the television station. We think your brother and your two sons are already dead. We think your wife is being hidden in Kenya. You understand, don't you, why I can't offer military assistance?"

China. One of the most powerful Authoritarian states in the modern world. And the military coup – too often the Authoritarian's chosen method for asserting his dominance. With these two examples, *The West Wing* powerfully frames the Authoritarian menace.

In most primate cultures, the alpha male rules.

A single individual, more powerful than his peers, governs the group by means of strength and intimidation, and in the process inculcates fear in others, takes females at will, and enjoys the highest level of privilege – until toppled from power by a superior challenger. So the story goes, among apes and throughout human history.

The assumption is that we naturally conform to this 'alpha' framework of authority.

But if we are more bonobo than chimpanzee, it no longer makes sense; and if we truly are off course, socially – having screwed up millennia of cooperative social order when we ceased to be migratory – then the idea of alpha humans no longer makes sense.

This is what we're talking about when we invoke the term *authoritarianism*. It is used in both political science (to describe the political orientation of a nation-state) and psychology (to describe the dynamics of leader-and-follower, where Authoritarianism is the rule). It does not differ significantly, in social terms, from what we observe in chimpanzees.

And when it took hold of humankind, it took hold big: for many thousands of years, our sociopolitical systems have been far more Authoritarian than not.

Authoritarianism strips the individual of self-determination. By centralizing authority in an individual, it strips the group of the benefit of pooled knowledge and decision-making skills. By awarding group rule according to personal power, rather than according to actual leadership merits, it represents a danger to the group that amplifies over time.

The Authoritarian regimes that have come and gone over the millennia that human beings have been civilized are countless. Even in the modern era, the age of democracy, Authoritarianism continues to rise up, threatening to return us to a sociopolitically captive state.

This couldn't have happened in the Paleolithic. Human survival hinged on multiple axes, not just one: the group required the leadership of a long-term planner, able to anticipate environmental conditions and food supplies months in advance; adept pattern-finders were needed, individuals able to sense weather change and changes in the behavior of prey; and fast-response captains were needed, in moments of sudden attack from predators.

That's not a single leader – that's several, each with a different skill set...a different cognitive style.

Among chimpanzees, Authoritarian leadership limits the tribe; it is not able to organize beyond swarming on prey and internal power struggle. It is a constant competition for the top spot, with no attention to the social development of the tribe.

Among the bonobos, leadership is distributed, as it is in democracies. No one individual member of the tribe holds absolute power, and anyone who tries is rapidly slapped down.

Put simply: when we enabled Authoritarianism, we were stepping backward, not forward – and we created a danger that threatens us today, possibly more than it ever has before.

What the expert says

The pacesetter in the academic study of Authoritarianism is Bob Altemeyer, retired professor of psychology at the University of Manitoba. The most aggressive investigator of Authoritarianism for more than three decades, Altemeyer's books on the subject are essential reading for any who would undertake its study.

Long established in academic circles, Altemeyer came to national attention when his explanation of Authoritarian behaviors in American politics made their way into the polemics of John Dean (of Watergate fame). At Dean's urging, Altemeyer wrote a book on the subject for laypeople.[1]

Altemeyer has, not surprisingly, had a great deal to say about Donald Trump.

"Authoritarian followers in America today are tremendously energized by fear and anger," he wrote in March 2016. "They're scared, and they want someone really strong and confident to protect them. It's a very natural, understandable reaction.

"Wanna-be tyrants in a democracy are just comical figures on soapboxes when they have no following. So the real threat lay coiled in parts of the population itself, it was thought, ready someday to catapult the next Hitler to power with their votes."

His explanation of the thinking of Authoritarian followers illuminates their choice of Donald Trump:

"Research suggests that 20-25% of the adults in North America are highly vulnerable to a demagogue who would incite hatred of various minorities to gain power. These people are waiting for a tough "man on horseback" who will supposedly solve all our problems through the ruthless application of force. When such a man gains prominence, you can expect the Authoritarian followers to mate devotedly with the Authoritarian leader, because each gives the other something they desperately want: the feeling of safety for the followers, and the tremendous power of the modern state for the leader.

Not all Trump voters qualify as Authoritarian followers, Altemeyer wrote, "but they likely compose his hard-core base. Furthermore, many Authoritarian followers [supported] Senator Ted Cruz for religious reasons." He went on to predict "most of them [will] slide into the Trump ranks once Cruz drops out of the race. By summer [2016], the vast majority of authoritarian followers in the United States will likely be for Trump."

Which, of course, is exactly what happened.

As for what happens next, "If you believe that a President Trump would be a very stiff test of democracy in the United States, then what can you do?... Well, it's not going to be easy changing highly aggressive, dogmatic, insular people who will dismiss you out of hand as the enemy... they have been that way for most of their lives, and they have built a lot of supports, including straight-out denial, to keep their views intact.

"One suspects they will feel even more betrayed if... [Trump] turns out to have been conning them all along, too. But he is going to keep telling them he's one of them, and keep them scared and angry while selling himself as the Toughest Guy They Ever Met. Authoritarian followers are always waiting for The Leader, and now they firmly believe they've found him."

Here's a list of traits Altemeyer observes in Authoritarian followers:

1. They are highly ethnocentric, highly inclined to see the world as their in-group versus everyone else. Because they are so committed to their in-group, they are very zealous in its cause.
2. They are highly fearful of a dangerous world. Their parents taught them, more than parents usually do, that the world is dangerous. They may also be genetically predisposed to experiencing stronger fear than most people do.
3. They are highly self-righteous. They believe they

are the "good people" and this unlocks a lot of hostile impulses against those they consider bad.

4. They are aggressive. Given the chance to attack someone with the approval of an authority, they will lower the boom.

5. They are highly prejudiced against racial and ethnic minorities, non-heterosexuals, and women in general.

6. Their beliefs are a mass of contradictions. They have highly compartmentalized minds, in which opposite beliefs exist side-by-side in adjacent boxes. As a result, their thinking is full of double standards.

7. They reason poorly. If they like the conclusion of an argument, they don't pay much attention to whether the evidence is valid or the argument is consistent.

8. They are highly dogmatic. Because they have gotten their beliefs mainly from the authorities in their lives, rather than think things out for themselves, they have no real defense when facts or events indicate they are wrong. So they just dig in their heels and refuse to change.

9. They are very dependent on social reinforcement of their beliefs. They think they are right because almost everyone they know, almost every news broadcast they see, almost every radio commentator they listen to, tells them they are. That is, they screen out the sources that will suggest that they are wrong.

10. Because they severely limit their exposure to different people and ideas, they vastly overestimate the extent to which other people agree with them.

11. And thinking they are "the moral majority"

supports their attacks on the "evil minorities" they
see in the country.

12. They are easily duped by manipulators who
pretend to espouse their causes when all the con
artists really want is personal gain.

13. They are largely blind to themselves. They have
little self-understanding and insight into why they
think and do what they do.

Altemeyer's Global Change Game

Altemeyer writes of some experiments he conducted with a
team in 1994. They involved the Global Change Game, a
simulation of international-level interactions between groups
of students, meant to explore issues affecting the planet and
humankind as a whole.

The game is played on a map the size of a basketball court.
A group of 70 students or so play the game together, each
assigned to one of 10 regions of the world, representing 100
million people. Assets are distributed among the regions, and
each has its own set of issues to deal with: health, hunger,
deforestation, climate change, energy shortages, encroaching
desert, economic instability, international trade, inequality –
all of these and more can appear on the horizon of any world
region.

Three of the regions are nuclear superpowers. Conventional
military power is distributed as it is in the real world, and
several start off the game with indigenous poverty – again, as
in the real world. Facilitators (faculty members) present each
region with problems, and it is left to the teams in each region
to reach out to request or offer aid, to enter into alliances, to
band together to solve problems or oppose one another and
create new ones.

Several of the students declare themselves "Elites" – leaders
– and the game allows for such players to squirrel away some

of their region's wealth for themselves.

Regions can enter into trade agreements, take in refugees, pollute the oceans, offer humanitarian aid, screw up the world economy, and even declare nuclear war (which ends the game by default). After 40 simulated years of international activity, the game is declared over, and points are tallied to determine the winning region.

The Low-Authoritarians

Altemeyer's innovation was to populate one night's run of the game purely with students who had scored low on his RWA scale – students low in Authoritarianism (the students were not made aware that their RWA scores had anything to do with the game). These students managed to achieve world peace and international cooperation. The 10 Elites (seven men, three women) joined together on Tasmania whenever a crisis arose and solved the problem together.

The three nuclear superpowers chose to disarm, and no war broke out during the playing of the game. An ozone depletion crisis was solved with the combined economic support of the wealthiest nations and advanced technology. There were several hundred million deaths resulting from disease and starvation in poverty-stricken countries (Europe sent aid – North America refused). World population at the end of the game was 8.7 billion, but resources were distributed worldwide in such a way as to support almost all of them. Overall, Altemeyer considered it a great success.

The High-Authoritarians

The following night, the game was repeated – this time with students who had all scored high on the Authoritarian scale. The Elites (all male) declined to disarm, and instead began heavy militarization. The Middle East region immediately doubled oil prices. The Soviet Union prepared to invade North America. A nuclear exchange followed soon after, ending the game.

The facilitators turned off the lights and described the effects of nuclear winter to the students before restarting the game. This time, the Soviet Union invaded China, killing 400 million. The Elite from the Middle East called a United Nations meeting, but nothing came of it.

The ozone depletion crisis occurred, but no cooperative activity was attempted. The European region made some independent efforts to reduce emissions, but the problem got steadily worse. Poverty and population growth went unchecked around the world. Rather than address their nation's economic challenges, the Elites maneuvered for personal power. Alliances were formed, with stronger partners forcing weaker ones to buy in.

At the end of 40 simulated years, the planet was coming apart, facing mounting crises, armed to the teeth and ready for holocaust. A total of 1,700 million people were dead. The Elites had plundered their regions for personal wealth.

And these were college students!

"There they were, in a big room full of people *just like themselves*, and they all turned their backs on each other and paid attention only to their own group," Altemeyer wrote later. "They too were all reading from the same page, but write large on their page was, 'Care About Your Own; We Are NOT All In This Together'."

The implications of these experiments are staggering. These two groups of students varied *only* in their test scores on the Right-Wing Authoritarian Scale; in every other way, they were typical college students, ages 18-22, predominantly white, middle-class, with age-appropriate concerns.

Yet when faced with the opportunity to cooperate or enter into conflict, their differing levels of Authoritarianism caused them to behave entirely differently.

Think about that for a moment. If that can happen in two evenings of game play among young people, it is no surprise to see what we see in the world around us today and throughout history, when power is placed in the hands of adults with these same tendencies and impulses.

Altemeyer and the Authoritarian mind

Most of the contents of the Authoritarian mind have come under Altemeyer's scrutiny. In his dozens of studies over the years, he has made use of many instruments, measuring everything from ethnocentricity to dogmatism to logical fallacy. The collective result is a remarkably sharp image of that mind, one that will be familiar to anyone who has that belligerent Fox News-watching uncle who can't shut up about what he heard yesterday on talk radio.

Altemeyer isn't the only one. A number of social scientists have conducted studies investigating the personality features that seem to define Authoritarians. They collectively form a cognitive portrait that is both familiar and remarkably consistent.

Prejudice and bigotry

Altemeyer developed an instrument for measuring an individual's level of ethnocentrism, the Manitoba Ethnocentrism Scale. Subjects rate the truth or falsehood of statements about members of other ethnicities on a scale of -4 to +4, yielding an index of ethnocentric orientation that can be correlated with results on other instruments, such as his RWA scale. In repeated experiments in both Canada and the United States, subjects who scored high on one strongly tended to score high on the other.

He noted that Authoritarian followers who were prejudiced against one ethnic group tended to be prejudiced toward them all – and toward other out-groups, such as homosexuals, as well (this finding has long been established by social psychologists). "Authoritarian followers dislike so many kinds of people, I have called them 'equal opportunity bigots'."

As mentioned in the chapter "A Sociopolitical Family Portrait", Authoritarians are often religious fundamentalists. It's an identity marker, Altemeyer noted, and that reinforced the Authoritarian Us, as noted in the chapter "Authoritarian 'Us' v. Egalitarian 'Them'". He put all of this together in yet another instrument, the Religious Ethnocentrism Scale.

The scale measures the degree to which the subject feels their religion should be the national religion; the degree to which other religions should be ignored; the undesirability of mixing with those with differing beliefs, and so on. For good measure, is also measures the subject's level of disagreement with statements stressing the equality of different religions and the worthiness of religious Others. Unsurprisingly, high-RWAs who identified as fundamentalist Christians scored high in religious ethnocentrism.

Then Altemeyer went a step further, wondering if those who did score high on the Ethnocentrism scale were open to this truth about themselves. He added a question to the test, asking the subject if they would wish to know their score if it turned out it showed them to be highly prejudiced?

In one such experiment, 76% of the low-RWA subjects said they would want to know their score; only 55% of the high-RWAs wanted to know. Then, for clarification, he reversed the question, in a subsequent experiment: the final question asked if the subject if they would wish to know their score if it awarded them a *low* score? The low-RWA subjects scored about the same – 71%; but this time, 77% of the high-RWAs wanted to know their score. Conclusion: low-RWAs are equally interested in good or bad news about themselves, while high-

RWAs are very open to good news but less open to bad.

Altemeyer's curiosity was derived from noting that highly prejudiced people tend to deny being so. This lack of self-awareness, he concluded, was essentially tribal: "If you spend a lot of time around rather prejudiced people," he wrote, "you can easily think your own prejudices are normal."

Why some people love Authoritarians

I've written in the past that Authoritarianism is not necessarily a good thing or a bad thing in and of itself, but becomes constructive or destructive depending on the social context in which it presents.

I hope I've gotten better at writing about the subject and conveying the key ideas, because we're living in an increasingly Authoritarian world, and that's not a good thing, and it's important to talk about it openly and frequently. To that end, I've discovered a short video of exceptional clarity that explains the subject concisely, yet insightfully. The YouTube link to the video is given below.

I want to summarize its contents, but before I do that, I'll briefly recap the pros and cons of Authoritarianism and its opposite, Egalitarianism.

Authoritarian personalities tend to:

- Desire strong leadership
- Obey authority
- Favor hierarchical social order
- Abhor uncertainty
- Resist change
- Feel unsafe, in a wide range of circumstances
- Believe in zero-sum scenarios
- Be very loyal
- Contribute generously to the well-being of the tribe

For context, let's remember that egalitarian personalities tend to:

- Prefer decision-by-consensus to the leadership of an individual
- Embrace change
- Seek novelty
- Take risks
- Distrust authority
- Be more loyal to ideas than to people
- Be more comfortable with uncertainty
- Favor an equal, distributed social order
- Contribute generously to the well-being of the tribe)

Taken as a whole, it's easy to see that all of these traits potentially have considerable merit in a community; there is room for all of them, and a role for every member, whichever traits they possess.

In Paleolithic societies, individuals with the Authoritarian traits listed above (remember, these are ultimately genetic personality and behavioral factors, not political or ideological distinctions) would have made a good Fire-Tender – a person who could be counted on to safeguard the tribe through the long night by keeping the bonfire going, to discourage attacks by predators.

But we are not living in the Paleolithic Era anymore. And the *mis*-application of Authoritarian tendencies, given our utterly different modern context, can be catastrophic. A modern Authoritarian may tend to:

- Submit to an unworthy leader simply because they make them feel safe;
- Be vulnerable to manipulation by way of falsehoods triggering fear responses;
- Accept misinformation about those in other tribes

designed to render them "dangerous" or "enemies";
- Believe in zero-sum scenarios (where there must be a loser for every winner) without justification, creating a false defensiveness;
- Be dismissive of facts, data, reason, logic, and evidence, when they challenge ideas or beliefs that promote an emotional feeling of safety and security;
- Be willing to suspend equality and fairness, and become accepting of unethical behavior in a leader, if feelings of dread or danger are present.

And this describes what we see all around us, of course, most every day today. Authoritarianism is commonplace; its disciples are numerous. And there is no shortage of social dominators waiting to exploit them.

Now, to the video. It can be found here, if you wish to check it out yourself:

https://www.youtube.com/watch?v=qw8yJ92c_Ds

It opens with the citing of a 2017 National Academy of Sciences study, "Dominant Leader vs. Prestige Leader", which found that people living in zip codes with a history of economic hardship were more likely to support Authoritarian leaders in their communities.

It then cites another 2017 study from CNBC, "Why Voters Might Be Choosing Authoritarian Leaders", a three-decade inquiry that surveyed people all over the world, finding that people tend to lean toward Authoritarian leaders in times of economic uncertainty – and that in such times, they are more likely to accept the suspending of democratic norms and to be more tolerant of unethical behavior in their leaders.

It notes a study on Pacific Standard, "The Terrifying Trait That Trump Triggers", which quantifies Authoritarians of making up roughly one-third of the populations of 29 different democracies around the world, but that in such countries, the tendencies of these Authoritarians tend to remain dormant until triggered by some threat (real or perceived). This brings us to the conclusion that it is not that economic uncertainty or other social threats cause people to become Authoritarian, but that 1/3 of the population already possesses Authoritarian tendencies, and threats will cause those tendencies to emerge.

The video explains that the Authoritarian mindset is all-pervasive, not just a batch of situational responses. Authoritarians, for instance, prioritize certain qualities in their children over others – obedience, good manners, and good behavior over independence, curiosity, and critical thinking.

Finally, the video noted that a 2017 *Politico Magazine* study, "Predicting Whether You're a Trump Supporter", reported that an Authoritarian mindset was the sole statistically significant variable predictive of Trump support.

In our current national moment, we see that Authoritarians seem impervious to all inputs from anyone *but* the strongman leaders they follow: no amount of new information, data, facts, logic, or reason can penetrate their thinking. And this should be no surprise; they consider all such inputs to be suspect, efforts to subvert them, dangers to be resisted at all costs. Their emotional investment in the sense of safety and security they derive from their tribe supersedes everything else.

But we need people of *all* cognitive styles and mindsets in the world today, despite the dangers of those misapplied. Everyone has value, and everyone can contribute meaningfully. But an explicitly Authoritarian society under an explicitly Authoritarian strongman leader is the path to ruin: it will result in the loss of liberty, the proliferation of inequality, a landscape of manipulation and persecution. Authoritarianism must be kept in check.

The solution, per the video, is to support and promote those social policies that promote safety and stability, which reduce the triggering of Authoritarian responses – fair taxation, readily-available healthcare, affordable education, sustainable energy, free and fair elections. The presence of such resources promote feelings of safety and security, diminishing the threat posed by social dominators hoping to acquire power.

Rising Authoritarianism today

Authoritarianism is rising in the US today – and around the world. The intense interconnectedness of everything and everyone, enabled by the Internet and the social media it hosts, makes the work of Authoritarian leaders easier than it's ever been, and empowers those leaders to spray the disinformation, propaganda, and toxic rhetoric all over their followers like a firehose.

Even experts like Altemeyer are hard-pressed to produce a solution to this problem, though one ray of hope is that the mindset is largely biological; Authoritarianism is enabled in individual minds by a propensity for greater fear than most, combined with a lower level of social information processing. Those are genetically-linked brain features, making it probable that there's a limit to the number of Authoritarian-leaning minds in any given population. Statistics from around the world suggest that that number is roughly 35 percent.

It should also be clear to even the most casual observer of today's flame wars on social media that there is no talking an Authoritarian follower off the ledge. It is useless to argue with them, for all the reasons Altemeyer (and others) have articulated.

What's the *The West Wing* response here? A big part of it is the pursuit of cognitive diversity, already covered above; in a nutshell, the biggest step forward is to *break up or dilute social echo chambers everywhere you can.* Authoritarianism is weakened when diversity is strengthened.

Oh, and *vote...*

"I was just... I was wrong! Lots of times we don't know what's right or wrong, but lots of times we do, and come on, this is one!"

Integrity in the Public Square

Upon learning that his old friend and fellow soldier Kenny O'Neal has committed fraud in Pentagon procurements, Leo is in tears over what he feels is a staggering betrayal of the ethics he himself so firmly embraces.[38]

He shares the story of how Kenny saved his life in Vietnam with the President, and how others flew into enemy fire to get them out.

"Men died for us!" he almost sobs. "We had a responsibility to live our lives with integrity and honesty to honor their sacrifice!"

For having withheld the truth about his multiple sclerosis, President Bartlet faces a Congressional censure – which Leo

---

[38] In "An Khe", S5/E14.

very much does not want him to accept.[39]

In the end, though, he insists.

"No one in government takes responsibility for anything anymore," he tells Leo. "We foster, we obfuscate, we rationalize. 'Everybody does it.' That's what we say. So we come to occupy a moral safe house where everyone's to blame, so no one's guilty.

"*I'm* to blame. I was wrong!"

The importance of integrity

It is disheartening to live in an era when falsehood and intentional disinformation is not only ubiquitous, but fast becoming the rule. Three decades into the Internet and 15 years into the era of social media, we *expect* to be lied to constantly – even (and especially) by our leaders. We factor deceit into nearly even communication.

If we're to be successful in pushing back against rising Authoritarianism, we must build our worldview on positive, constructive agency in a world we feel responsible for improving. Lies and misinformation do not aid or promote that agency or improvement; they are gross impediments to it. To resist the Authoritarian, then, is to commit to integrity and truth in all one's actions and dealings, even though it means a dispirited slog through a daily morass of ugly falsehood.

Humanists are quick to publicly proclaim this commitment:

"We believe in the common moral decencies: altruism, integrity, honesty, truthfulness, responsibility," reads Paul Kurtz's "A Statement of Principles" in Free Inquiry's *Affirmations of Humanism*. "Humanist ethics is amenable to

---

[39] In "H. Con-172", S3/E10.

critical, rational guidance. There are normative standards that we discover together. Moral principles are tested by their consequences."

"We believe in optimism rather than pessimism," he continues, "hope rather than despair, learning in the place of dogma, truth instead of ignorance, joy rather than guilt or sin, tolerance in the place of fear, love instead of hatred, compassion over selfishness, beauty instead of ugliness, and reason rather than blind faith or irrationality."

Scientific integrity as the model for truth

Committing to a non-magical, unwishful reality supported not only by the evidence of the senses but a foundation of sober reason leads many, if not most, into harmony with the method and findings of science. Empirical truth is generally accepted as the baseline for *all* truth; or, phrased antithetically, information or knowledge parading as truth that does *not* stand up to reason or empirical scrutiny is by its very nature suspect and likely to be rejected out of hand.

Liberals are not shy about stating this acceptance of science and its methods as truth-seeking. "Humanists embrace science as the most effective tool in understanding our reality," according to Andrew Copson. "Science values truth and looks for disagreement and debate to approach the truth more closely."

The American Humanist Association has formalized this embrace:

"The AHA considers the integrity of scientific knowledge, where information is assigned a degree of certainty according to the weight of the evidence, to be essential to a humanist society," it proclaims in its statement on Scientific Integrity.

"Humanists insist that scientific studies, peer-reviewed and reproduced in accordance with the highest standards, be the basis for public policy and education. Religious or sectarian doctrine is irrelevant and immaterial to discerning best practices."

It's worth a brief recap to remind ourselves exactly what this commitment entails.

Per the scientific method, for a new idea or theory to be accepted as fact, it must

- be thoroughly examined in an objective manner;
- be dispassionately tested via a method that can reveal its potential falsity;
- be subjected to intensive efforts to disprove it;
- endure repeated testing by others, to validate the correctness of its analysis

Then, and only then, can this new idea or information be accepted as fact.

Again, antithetically, the proclamations of those in authority do not become factual just because they are spoken by those in authority (this discounts almost everything offered by our current leaders).

The knowledge of the masses, no matter how universally embraced, isn't real knowledge solely on the basis of their broad acceptance.

And new ideas do not become credible or worthy of designation of fact simply because they are exciting, intriguing, or emotionally pleasing.

This means that new information we want to take on board as real must not only run the gauntlet of scientific scrutiny, but must swim upstream through the yowls of the crowd, the bellowing of the powerful and our own susceptibility to wishful thinking.

The liberal's attitude toward truth then, can be summed up as follows: you gotta want it bad, because the information streams of our current society are gonna put up a fight.

But liberals *do* want it bad. The liberal treasures truth and integrity, and science was invented explicitly to deliver them. Here are some excerpts from the American Humanist Association's Resolution on Scientific Integrity:

WHEREAS the power for human progress resident in modern science, when used and controlled democratically, offers a method for the establishment of peace on a global scale;

WHEREAS the outcomes of our actions are predicted by scientific methods and play a key role in our ethical decisions;

WHEREAS scientific leaders require the professional integrity to identify a level of certainty to all claims, distinguishing between tentative and conclusive findings;

BE IT RESOLVED in furtherance of human flourishing, the American Humanist Association

AFFIRMS that the methods of science be relied upon in assessing the efficacy of our actions and policies to bring about stated ethical outcomes;

AFFIRMS that a skeptical approach to knowledge, assigning a level of certainty according to the weight of the evidence, is important to personal well-being;

DECRIES the elevation of ideological conviction or preconceived certainty over coherent theory, empirical observation, or expert peer review as determiners of truth;

DECRIES censorship, misinformation campaigns, and obstruction in the general populace, the Internet, or schools that subvert the process of free inquiry, dissemination of knowledge, or discovery of new information;

AFFIRMS that the advancement of scientific exploration and study must be tempered by humility, compassion, and constant care for all life and our environment.

Truth and integrity are not subject to whim; they do not indulge our wishes and wants; and they are certainly not in the purview of the powerful. Truth and integrity are non-negotiable. They are precious, and like anything we greatly prize, they are of tremendous value and ask of us a dear price.

It's a price we must willingly pay – an essential part of our resistance.

"A hundred years ago, a black guy couldn't show up at a club opening with a white girl for fear he'd be killed!"

Racism and Social Inequality

Zoey has been under heightened Secret Service protection since knowledge of her dating relationship with Charlie became public. They are supposed to attend a club opening together soon, but the Secret Service won't let them.[40]

A book about what American life was like a century in the past has been circulating through the West Wing. After receiving the news about having to cancel, Charlie bitterly reads aloud from it.

"Hey, look! It says here that a hundred years ago, a black guy couldn't show up to a club opening with a white girl for fear he'd be killed!"

In the Bartlet Administration transition, nominee for Attorney General Cornell Rooker turns out to be problematic.

---

[40] In "The White House Pro-Am", S1/E17.

CJ learns why when a writer for an Evangelical publication corners her in the press room:

"By the way - Just so you don't think we disagree on everything, I think Cornell Rooker is terrific," he tells her. "First African-American man I've ever heard make sense on racial profiling."[41]

The West Wing's stand against racism and social inequality may be the most overt of its many social stances. Instances of bigotry, featured as story points, stand out in high relief for their contrast to the principles of the Bartlet White House.

Racism and humanism

Racism and social inequality have been with us for millennia, of course; even the holy texts of the major ancient religions are teeming with it. They are such a human constant that it's easy to assume that they are built into human nature.

Today, we have a better understanding. Racism and social inequality are social phenomena, not natural phenomena. It can be safely said that there are no humanist organizations today that have not publicly renounced bigotry, racism, and other prejudicial behaviors, and to denounce instances of social inequality wherever they may be found.

Here are some examples:

"The principle of moral equality must be furthered through elimination of all discrimination based upon race, religion, sex, age, or national origin. This means equality of opportunity and recognition of talent and

---

41 In "Debate Camp", S4/E5.

merit. Individuals should be encouraged to contribute to their own betterment. ... We deplore racial, religious, ethnic, or class antagonisms. Although we believe in cultural diversity and encourage racial and ethnic pride, we reject separations which promote alienation and set people and groups against each other; we envision an integrated community where people have a maximum opportunity for free and voluntary association.

"At the present juncture of history, commitment to all humankind is the highest commitment of which we are capable; it transcends the narrow allegiances of church, state, party, class, or race in moving toward a wider vision of human potentiality. What more daring a goal for humankind than for each person to become, in ideal as well as practice, a citizen of a world community." ~11th Principle, Humanist Manifesto II

And this, from Humanists UK:

"Humanists condemn racism and racial discrimination in all its forms and are committed to campaigning for racial equality across all aspects of society. We have a positive track record throughout our existence in the fight for racial equality, from organising the first global race congress in 1911, to campaigning against colonialism in the early twentieth century, and for laws against racial discrimination from the mid-century. This commitment has continued through to today." ~Human Rights and Equality statement

And these excerpts from the Resolution on White Supremacy (American Humanist Association):

"*WHEREAS* white supremacy and the racism that sustains it remain particularized and systemic in our society, and

WHEREAS racism continues to limit the opportunities of and discriminate against racialized bodies of color in particular and marginalized bodies more generally, living in the United States by perpetuating inequality in every facet of individual and community life, and

WHEREAS hate crimes and hate groups have become more prevalent in the United States in recent years, especially targeting Black people, people perceived as Muslim, Jews, South Asians, LGBTQ people, and the disability community, and

WHEREAS dismantling white supremacy requires anti-racist action.

"*THEREFORE, BE IT RESOLVED* that the AMERICAN HUMANIST ASSOCIATION, in the pursuit of an anti-racist society,

AFFIRMS that all lives will matter when Black lives matter, and

AFFIRMS that economic justice for Black and Indigenous people requires federal policies that take drastic corrective measures to eradicate the racial wealth gap, and

AFFIRMS its support for anti-racist healthcare, including mental health services, that achieves the same health outcomes for Black and White people regardless of income, and

AFFIRMS its dedication to stamping out white supremacy and racism from within its organization through hiring practices, resource allocation, staff and board training, and more.

Per the humanist dynamic, it is of course not enough to take a political or philosophical position on racism; humanism calls for individual commitment and action. To that end, Samuel Kronen in "A Plea for a Humanist Antiracism" (in *Aero*, 2020) spells out some specifics:

> "A humanist antiracism would reject all racial double standards and express equal opprobrium at the police killings of both George Floyd and Tony Timpa. It would acknowledge the brutal legacy of historical racism, as well as the astounding racial progress made in the past half century, while never losing sight of how much further we have to go before race is irrelevant in public life. It would condemn racism in the strongest possible terms and root out what remains of it in our institutions, without suggesting that racism is responsible for everything that's unfair in society. It would reject notions of intergenerational bloodguilt and retributive justice. It would strive for a race-blind world without ignoring instances of persistent racial injustice. It would create more breathing room for conversations about race, by allowing us to see each other as human beings and not simply as avatars of our races. It would appreciate the real advantages and disadvantages experienced by certain groups and individuals in society without making a religion out of the notion of privilege. It would reject the tendency to make meaning out of race and use race as a proxy for underlying social conditions. It would focus on hard policy reform over symbolic gestures of piety. It would measure progress by comparing metrics of well-being to those of the past rather than in terms of racial disparities. And it would reject systematic discrimination, whether in the

form of overt racial quota systems in job applications and admissions procedures or subtle biases against blacks and other groups in policing, medicine and other sectors of American life."

Kronen's emphasis on social justice as the moving part in anti-racist action is echoed throughout the humanist communities and organizations of the world. Here's what the AHA says about it:

> "Humanists are naturally committed to social justice as a prerequisite to peace and happiness for the greatest number and see it as a moral failing to stand by while others are denied their civil and human rights. Humanistic social justice advocacy involves respect for the equality of all people, compassion for their dignity and welfare, and a conviction that positive change requires human intervention.

> "The AHA takes an intersectional view of social justice issues, recognizing that working to liberate all marginalized communities is the best way to lift the prospects of any one group. Humanism motivates us to act on a moral imperative to transform systems of oppression because they are incompatible with the aspirations of humanism.

> "Regardless of race, ethnicity, economic status, ability, sexual orientation, gender identity, religious beliefs or nonbelief, or citizenship, all individuals have universal human rights that must be respected and protected. Achieving global standards for human rights and international adherence to institutions such as the International Criminal Court and the United Nations

Universal Declaration of Human Rights facilitate enforcing individuals' rights the world over."

Racism today

In the US today, racism and social inequality have been on the rise, as right-wing politicians stir the animosities of white America with divisive rhetoric. Systemic racism has existed throughout the nation's existence, and social/economic inequality was the persistent companion of that racism until the 1950s. The Civil Rights Movement produced some gains – there are now black millionaires, black CEOs, even a black president – and access to higher education is now much easier for members of all ethnicities.

But there is still far to go. In a recent study conducted by Harvard's T.H. Chan School of Public Health, 57% of black Americans reported discrimination in pay and eligibility for promotion; 54% of Native Americans reported facing discrimination in hiring, promotion, and compensation.

The National Urban League reported in its 2022 annual report that, per the Equality Index, black Americans are only getting 73% as much of the American pie as white Americans; a black child born today can expect a life four years shorter, on average, than a white child; black women are 59% more likely to die while bearing a child than white women; 31% are more likely to die of breast cancer; black men are 52% more likely to die of prostate cancer.

According to a 2019 study by the Pew Research Center, 58% of Americans believe that racism in the nation is serious, and 56% believe that the Trump presidency made it worse. 51% of Americans believe that being Hispanic hinders a person's ability to succeed in the US. Among blacks themselves, 78% do not think enough has been done to address systemic racism in the US.

Regarding the expression of racist opinions and insensitive

views, 65% of Americans believe that expression became more common after Donald Trump became president; 45% said it has become more acceptable.

Among white Democrats, 64% say they do not believe the nation has done enough to address systemic racism; among white Republicans, the number is 15%. 80% of white Democrats say the legacy of slavery continues to impact American society today, while only 40% of white Republicans feel the same. And 78% of white Democrats say the problem is people not seeing racism where it exists, while the same percentage of white Republicans say that people see racial discrimination where it really isn't.

How we get Woke

Humanities Professor Anthony Pinn of Rice University gets more specific still, offering a list of Dos and Don'ts to apply when actively confronting racism:[2]

- **Don't make blanket statements concerning African-American involvement in theism.** "The relationship between African-Americans and Christianity is complex and layered," Pinn points out; in the African-American past, it pushed against injustice and helped produce a sense of identity and agency that worked against the dehumanization they were experiencing.
- **Don't assume humanism is a vaccine against poor thinking and poor behavior.** Humanists, Pinn asserts, are cultural creatures, and can be insensitive to racial injustice through the simple mechanism of believing that the logic they embrace elevates them beyond it.
- **Don't assume you get to set the racial justice agenda.** "You don't get to determine what are

appropriate markers of progress," Pinn writes; "your job is to promote solidarity, and to play the role assigned to you by those who are most directly and deeply impacted by issues of race and racism."

- **Do recognize the nature of privilege.** "Whiteness" comes with perks, Pinn states. There are forms of privilege that lurk in the background, to which the humanist should be alert: the assumption that the police are there to serve and protect, for instance, and the assumption that you weren't placed near the restroom in the restaurant because of the color of your skin.

- **Do educate yourself.** The serious humanist should put the same energy into learning about matters of race, Pinn insists, that they put toward learning about separation of church and state, evolution, and other important humanist issues.

- **Do recognize difference as an opportunity.** Difference, per Pinn, is "an opportunity... a chance to add complexity to a community and to learn from approaches and perspectives outside what is considered normative. It's an opportunity to appreciate what has been considered marginal to U.S. life and to understand its actual centrality. In a certain way, difference as opportunity points to the need to appreciate cultural diversity, learn from it, and embrace possibilities that push us beyond the familiar and comfortable."

All pretty Woke, isn't it? Well... *The West Wing* is nothing if not Woke.

LGBTQ

A teenager named Lowell Lydell is in critical condition after having been accosted by other children for being gay. Leo informs CJ about it:[42]

"He got beaten up, then they stripped him naked, tied him to a tree and threw rocks and bottles at his head," Leo reports. "You know how old the assailants were? Thirteen."

In the Right's War on Woke, there are few issues as venomous as sexual orientation. People who don't conform to a white, Christian view of the bedroom seem to make them disturbingly uncomfortable.

This is no surprise. Long before the word "woke" came along – long before "conservative" and "liberal" became sociopolitical designations – Authoritarian and patriarchal personalities have bristled and howled over people who do not conform to their notions of correct and proper sexuality. We don't have to look further than the Old Testament to realize this way of thinking has been with us for thousands of years.

This does not fully explain, however, the anti-Woke crowd's laser-sharp targeting of LGBTQ people at this particular moment in history. So intense has these attacks become that they echo the Right's war on the environment: they despise pro-LGBTQ policy so deeply that they vigorously assault businesses who deploy it – even though the pro-LGBTQ policies are good for business, and (on paper) they themselves are pro-business.

Here are some examples:

---

[42] In "In Excelsis Deo", S1/E10.

- Per a report in *Forbes*, when Woolworths tweeted support for International Pride Month, expressing commitment to their LGBTQ customers, conservative outrage ensued; Woolworth's doubled down, tweeting that "every person has the right to dignity, regardless of their identity; this is a fact enshrined in our constitution, it is not up for debate";
- Similar conservative outrage erupted in New Zealand, when The Warehouse retail outlet sold items from the Disney pride collection;
- More of the outrage emerged over *Glamour UK*, which featured a picture of pregnant transgender man Logan Broan on its cover;
- According to the *Dallas Morning News*, Southwest Airlines has been forced to deal with a website and local billboard smearing it as "Southwoke" for its promotion of racial and LGBTQ diversity;
- Target bowed to similar anti-Woke pressure, pulling LGBTQ items from its Pride collection when workers' safety was threatened, according to the *Washington Post*;
- The *New York Times* reported that Anheuser-Busch made a similar retreat in the face of conservative boycotts following TikTok star Dylan Mulvaney's promotion of a beer contest; two of the company's top executives were put on leave, and the company announced that its future marketing would focus on sports and music.

"Recent pushback against businesses such as Anheuser-Busch and Target, blatantly organized by extremist groups, serves as a wake up call for all businesses that support the LGBTQ+ community," read a statement from the Human Rights Campaign. "We've seen this extremist playbook of attacks before. Their goal is clear: to prevent LGBTQ+ inclusion and representation, silence our allies and make our community invisible."

As with the rage over businesses treating the environment responsibly, this behavior makes no economic sense: the asset management group LGBT Capital estimates that the annual purchasing power of the global LGBTQ community is $3.9 trillion. No business in its right mind would turn its back on such a broad customer base.

It's not just the assault on business; worse than that is the assault on law.

The Republican governor of Florida, Ron DeSantos, has become the public face of the anti-LGBTQ Right, with two major bills that have received national attention and scrutiny: an "anti-woke" bill and the "Don't Say Gay" bill. Both are designed to dictate what teachers can and cannot say in classrooms. The first presents a list of race-related concepts that are forbidden in lessons for students; the second prohibits discussion of sexual orientation and gender identity in grade school classrooms. The irony in the latter case, of course, is that teachers were not presenting those topics to children of that age in the first place, suggesting that the law is pure political posturing.

At the federal level, anti-LGBTQ legislation has been surfacing in must-pass funding bills in the House of Representatives, with Republican lawmakers embedding 45 such provision in those bills in an attempt to weaken discrimination protections for same-sex couples and restrict gender-affirming care. Several appropriations bills include provisions for the restriction of gender transition care for those on Medicare, Medicaid, and ACA-subsidized plans. They would also impact trans members of the military and their dependents, as well as federal employees. There are also provisions for the banning of Pride flags over government buildings, the nullification of protections for same-sex couples, and restriction of funding of programs promoting diversity and inclusion.

Down in Texas, the Republican Party has formally defined homosexuality as an "abnormal lifestyle choice" and openly stated its opposition to "all efforts to validate transgender identity." The party platform includes a call to repeal the 1965 Voting Rights Act, as well as a statement that LGBTQ people should not be legally protected from discrimination. It further states that being gay or trans is a choice.

"We believe there should be no granting of special legal entitlements or creation of special status for homosexual behavior, regardless of state of origin, and we oppose any criminal or civil penalties against those who oppose homosexuality out of faith, conviction, or belief in traditional values," it reads.

Texas Republicans have also called for a ban on gender-affirming care.

In 2022, more than 300 anti-LGBTQ bills were pending in state legislatures. According to the Human Rights Campaign, at least six states have banned transgender women and girls from competing on sports teams consistent with their gender. Alabama, Arizona and Texas have taken steps to ban gender-affirming care for young people; in Alabama, it is now a felony for a doctor to provide such care to minors. Other states are also following Florida's lead, introducing bills that mimic "Don't Say Gay".

Three states now have laws in place preventing trans children from accessing care for gender dysphoria, even when recommended by major medical associations. Two have outlawed discussion of LGBTQ history or individuals in classrooms.

And then there are the Christians...

Randall Balmer, a professor at Dartmouth who grew up in an Evangelical household, offers some perspective on the breathtaking surge in LGBTQ hatred, noting that much of it comes from Evangelicals. The point of it all, he has written, is to keep that community mobilized as a voting block for the Right.[1]

"They have an interest in keeping the base riled up about one thing or another, and when one issue fades, as with same-sex relationships and same-sex marriage, they've got to find something else," Balmer said in an interview with *The 19th*. "It's almost frantic."

His research traces this methodology to Paul Weyrich, one of the founders of the Religious Right, in the Seventies. Weyrich began testing issues that would drive Evangelicals to the voting booth, and this became a standard practice, permanently installing white Evangelicals as the key factor in Republican wins.

Once gay marriage was settled, much to the Religious Right's chagrin, "they almost frantically began looking for something else," Balmer said. "And of course, the trans thing was the next thing on the horizon."

What the public thinks

What does the general public think of all this? Unsurprisingly, there's a clear partisan divergence: 3/4ths of Republicans say the US should promote traditional values, and 2/3rds of Democrats support greater tolerance of diversity. Independents are split down the middle.

That poll gets more granular, asking very specific questions about tolerance from a public policy viewpoint:

- Government should promote greater respect for traditional values: 27% (D), 65% (R)
- Government should promote greater tolerance of people with different lifestyles: 66% (D), 18% (R)

- US should increase social justice: 66% (D), 21% (R)
- The country should reduce political correctness and cancel culture: 19% (D), 67% (R)
- Promotion of LGBTQ lifestyle and values has gone too far: 12% (D), 70% (R)
- The US should be more accepting of the LGBTQ community: 60% (D), 10% (R)

US voters across the political spectrum acknowledge that the surge in anti-LGBTQ legislation is political theater more than moral conviction. In a 2023 Data for Progress survey, those who think there is "too much" legislation aimed at "limiting the rights of transgender and gay people in America" include 64% of voters in general; 72% of Democrats, 65% of Independents, and 55% of Republicans.

General support for marriage equality is now around 70%, with PRRI's 2022 American Values Atlas noting that same-sex marriage support is at 60% or greater in 43 states.

Per the non-partisan Public Religion Research Institute, almost 80% of Americans support protections against discrimination for LGBTQ people (this even includes 65% of Republicans). A 2021 PBS Newshour/NPR/Marist poll reported that 2/3[rd]s of Americans oppose bills that limit transgender rights.

We've already noted in the broader discussion of diversity above that our differences make human community stronger, an idea that *The West Wing* emphasized again and again. Increasing diversity and tolerance, and pushing back against attacks on both, is not only noble; it's a means of improving our collective capability and accelerating human progress. It is worthy of our deep commitment and investment.

The past few decades of American life have demonstrated what honest, self-aware people have known all along: skin color makes no difference; gender makes no difference. And neither does sexual orientation. It's as *West Wing* to support the LGBTQ community as it is to support racial and gender equality.

"This is a country where women aren't allowed to drive a car. They're not allowed to be in the company of any man other than a close relative, they're required to adhere to a dress code that would make a Maryknull Nun look like Malibu Barbie."

Rights and Freedoms

CJ frequently comments on the plight of women in extreme Islamic nations, and Josh gives voice to their lack of rights in a discussion of Islam with a group of high school students in the White House mess. Islamic women, he tells them, "are not allowed to attend school or have jobs. They're not allowed to be unaccompanied, and oftentimes get publicly stoned to death for crimes like not wearing a veil."[43]

---

[43] In "Isaac and Ishmael", S3/E0.

Most of the pushback against Woke in the US is about rights – human rights, civil rights, political rights, economic rights, social rights, cultural rights. If you're Woke, you generally believe that these rights, and the freedoms they enshrine, should be available to all; if you're not Woke, you generally believe that some people should have fewer rights than others.

The tendency of the anti-Woke to attack some specific groups – LGBTQ, for instance – is examined above. But the general pushback against equal rights for all exists over and above specific attacks on specific groups; it is founded on a belief, held by far too many, that some people are better or more worthy than others.

That belief flies in the face of democracy, of course; but the staggering depth of the chasm between the Woke view on rights and freedoms and the view of Woke's opposition is truly commitment to two separate realities.

> *"The basic tool for the manipulation of reality is the manipulation of words. If you can control the meaning of words, you can control the people who must use the words."*
>
> *~Philip K. Dick*

The dual realities we find ourselves confronting is based on two completely different meanings of the word *freedom*.

The point of rights is to secure freedoms; attacks on the rights of any particular group are an attempt to restrict or remove that group's freedoms. Defense of those rights, conversely, are attempts to preserve those freedoms.

What freedoms are we talking about?

If you're Woke, those include freedom from persecution over sexual orientation, gender identity, skin color or ethnicity. You support equal rights for persons in these groups, and expect the government to enforce those rights. 'We the People', to you, means people of all colors, ethnic origins, religions, and sexual persuasions.

If you aren't, *freedom* doesn't mean rights shared by all, enforced by the government; it means freedom *from* government.

This idea has been in the US water supply for more than a century, but it took root in the public gestalt with the election of Ronald Reagan to the White House in 1980. It was a coup for a particular cabal of economists, politicians, and businessmen – disciples of *neoliberalism*.

Neoliberalism and freedom

The neoliberal agenda is vast, but its central tenets are easily summarized:

- The US government is your enemy;
- The government needs to get out of the business of helping average Americans;
- The well-being of business transcends the national interest;
- *Deregulate, deregulate, deregulate!*

Ronald Reagan was a neoliberal juggernaut on all these fronts, setting the tone and strategy for all in the GOP who would follow him.

His assaults on the democratic order weren't just systematic and persistent; they were overt, out in the open, often paraded on national television.

"Government is not the solution to our problem, government *is* the problem," he declared, followed later by, "The nine most terrifying words in the English language are: 'I'm from the government, and I'm here to help.'" – casually vilifying, at a stroke, the hundreds of thousands who *do* enter public service out of a deep desire and conviction to help others and contribute to the betterment of the nation.

Reagan's demonization of government, already a GOP staple, was perhaps the least of it; his valentine to capitalism, a gutting of tax policy that had been in place since World War II, requiring businesses and the very wealthy to contribute their fair share back to the economy that had enriched them, exploded the national debt. In cutting the top tax rate from 70% to 25%, he tripled that debt, from $738 billion to $2.4 trillion. That quickly, the US went from being the world's largest creditor to the world's largest debtor.

The justification was that the US economy wasn't functioning properly, but that wasn't true at all. The economy had boomed steadily during the post-World War II years, with only the normal fluctuations. The number of people in the US living in poverty had continually declined, even as the overall population rose.

In the process, Reagan and his allies laid track for the GOP to come by dissembling in the media to justify his agenda. His budget director, David Stockman, perpetuated the trickle-down gospel that cutting taxes on corporations and the wealthy would trigger large returns as the savings would be re-invested in the economy, in effect paying for the cuts. The Office of Management and Budget debunked this myth with actual analysis, prompting Stockman to confess publicly that "None of us really understands what's going on with all these numbers... the whole thing is premised on faith, on a belief about how the world works."

'Trickle-down' wasn't real economic theory; it was conservative, neoliberal ideology. And when Stockman later said publicly that the tax cuts really were, in fact, a valentine to business, calling the whole thing a 'Trojan horse', he was castigated by the president.

Forty years later, 'trickle-down' has yet to function as promised, even though the current crop of GOP politicians continue to shop it; the money the uber-wealthy are saving on their tax bills isn't and never has been re-invested in the economy. It sits in off-shore accounts.

A firestorm of deregulation followed the tax cuts, stagnating the prosperity of the middle class as the growth of the minimum wage dropped away and economic inequality surged. The push for privatization of government began in earnest, sending healthcare costs into the stratosphere, and barriers to the exporting of US manufacturing to nations where labor was far cheaper evaporated. The export of US manufacturing to other countries, gutting the domestic jobs market as it dismantled unions, was accompanied by a breathtaking surge in the trade deficit. Reagan inherited from Carter a deficit of only $13 billion; when he left office, it had soared to a mind-blowing $685 billion.

Perhaps most damning was the elimination of the Fairness Doctrine in 1987. The policy that had protected the integrity of public information since the dawn of radio was dropped, enabling the wild-west, anything-goes parade of disinformation and outright deception that clogs up media today. The airwaves ceased to be conduits for news and became what they are today – ideology pipelines.

Neoliberalism was off and running. The global, regulation-free landscape for the cultivation of wealth envisioned by Milton Friedman and his cohorts was finally taking shape. The transformation of the US government from the middle-class-building, consumer-protecting, civil-rights-promoting agency it had become since the New Deal into capitalism's passive enabler was well underway.

Reaganism was indeed a Trojan horse, and the forces it unleashed have ended or endangered many of the institutions we thought would last forever. Civil discourse in the conducting of the people's business is long gone; inequality has surged; people no longer trust those they count on to protect them. Deceit has been normalized, the rule of law is precarious, and violence – even murder! – in pursuit of political ends is becoming acceptable on US soil.

All so Elon Musk can go to Mars.

Born in the South

Historian Heather Cox Richardson reminds us that this way of thinking goes back to the Civil War: the precursor to modern neoliberalism was the slave trade of the 19th century South, and the wealthy men who enabled it:

"The Thirteenth Amendment abolished human enslavement in the United States, except as punishment for a crime (an exception that later enabled the use of chain gangs). President Abraham Lincoln and the congressmen who embraced this monumental change to the Constitution expected that ending enslavement would end the power of a few elite southerners to dismantle the United States.

"Enslavement, they believed, had enabled a few men to monopolize wealth and power in the American South, where they dominated state governments and wrote laws to protect their own interests. Those same men had taken over first the Democratic Party and then the national government, controlling the Supreme Court, the Senate, and the presidency.

"The elite southerners insisted that the national government had no power to do anything that was not spelled out in the Constitution. It could protect the property interests of enslavers - through a law forcing free states to return escaped slaves, for example, or laws protecting enslavement in the western territories - but it could not do anything to help ordinary Americans, like dredging harbors, building roads, or establishing colleges, no matter how popular those measures might be.

"During the Civil War, Lincoln and his party rejected this old formula and created a new one. They pioneered a government that responded to the interests of ordinary Americans. Amending the Constitution to end enslavement was not simply an attempt to guarantee freedom for Black Americans; it was also designed to cement in place the government 'of the people, by the people, for the people.'

"Demonstrating that momentous change, the second section of the Thirteenth Amendment added: 'Congress shall have power to enforce this article by appropriate legislation.' The first ten amendments to the Constitution - the Bill of Rights - limited the power of the federal government. The Thirteenth was the first to expand it.

"[Lincoln and his supporters] knew that Black southerners supported this new government. They believed that poorer white southerners who had been crushed economically before the war as wealthy white enslavers gobbled up the region's best land and who had borne the brunt of the war would also embrace it. Under the new system, the North had defied all expectations and thrived during the war, and they thought its superiority to the old system was so obvious that ordinary southerners would jump at it.

"Many did... but white lawmakers in the southern

states did not. They agreed to ratify the Thirteenth Amendment, but enabled by President Andrew Johnson, who took over the presidency after Lincoln's assassination, they passed a series of laws that bound Black Americans to yearlong contracts working in white-owned fields, prohibited Black Americans from meeting together or owning guns, demanded that Black Americans behave submissively to white Americans, and sometimes punished white people who interacted with their Black neighbors.

"The *Chicago Tribune* wrote, 'The men of the North will turn the State of Mississippi into a frog-pond before they will allow any such laws to disgrace one foot of soil in which the bones of our soldiers sleep and over which the flag of freedom waves.' To counter these 'Black Codes,' Congress wrote the Fourteenth Amendment in 1866, and the states ratified it in 1868.

"Congress designed the Fourteenth Amendment to end forever the ability of state lawmakers to undermine the United States of America. The amendment declared anyone born or naturalized in the United States to be a U.S. citizen and then established the power of the federal government to stop states from discriminating against citizens. The Fourteenth Amendment establishes that states must treat everyone equally before the law, and they can't take away someone's rights without due process of the law."

The Civil War, then, provides us with a mirror in which to view our situation today: to the Woke North, *freedom* meant *freedom for both white and black*; to the anti-Woke South (the wealthy slaveowners, anyway), *freedom* meant *freedom from the federal government's interference in our right to take away the freedom of black people.*

'Twas ever thus. The Woke struggle is just another expression of a conflict that has burdened humankind since the invention of the idea of property: some believe they are more equal than others – and the wealthy, in particular, have been the ones to seize power whenever possible to secure their wealth by trimming away the power, rights, and freedoms of those others.

Operation Iraqi Freedom?

In another modern example, part of the Right's rhetoric over the conquest of Iraq in 2003 was that the invasion would democratize that nation – restore *freedom* to the Iraqi people. When President George Bush announced the invasion on March 19, 2003, he put a name to it: Operation Iraqi Freedom.

It's hard to imagine a greater irony, even from him.

"A peaceful world of growing freedom," Bush wrote on the first anniversary of 9/11, "serves American long-term interests, reflects enduring American ideals and unites America's allies. Humanity holds in its hands the opportunity to offer freedom's triumph over all its age-old foes... as the greatest power on Earth, we have an obligation to help the spread of freedom."

Reading those words, the average American would assume Bush meant we were invading Iraq to spread equal rights, to ensure the freedoms of all its citizens, regardless of their religion, color, sexual orientation, and so on. Like in America.

But, no; the *freedom* we were spreading was *neoliberalism*.

In September of the same year, Paul Bremer, head of the Coalition Provisional Authority, produced a series of orders to be implemented in the new Iraq:

- The full privatization of public enterprises;
- Full ownership rights, by foreign firms, of Iraqi businesses;
- The opening of Iraq's banks to foreign control;
- The elimination of all trade barriers.

Put another way, Iraq was to be *deregulated*.

On the other hand, what *would* be regulated – and heavily so - would be Iraqi workers themselves:

- Strikes were effectively forbidden in key sectors;
- The right to unionize was heavily restricted;
- A regressive flat tax would be imposed.

Iraqi was not to be made a *free* state in the sense that most Americans understand the term; it was to be made a *neoliberal* state, one that existed under conditions friendly to neoliberal visions of global markets.

When we wrap our heads around this appropriation of words and the imposition of very different meanings, we more clearly understand the staggering distance between Woke thought and convictions, and the thought and convictions of those who oppose it.

Governance as incentive

Conservatives, and neoliberals in particular, want to shrink government to the point they can drown it because they believe government is only good for one thing: protecting their property. All its other functions, particularly social functions, should be eradicated.

As they say that, they profess to be all for human flourishing, but that the *market* should be the source of that flourishing – not government.

The problem is, when people are flourishing, the wealthy can be counted on to find a way to exploit them. And the market can't do anything to stop them. Government is necessary to incentivize the proliferation of the freedoms that improve human well-being, because the market certainly doesn't; and, conversely, the government is necessary to *dis*-incentivize exploitation and the violation of the rights of others, by punishing those violations.

Other forces for Woke

We can imagine that the Bartlet Administration vision for America includes a universal manifesto articulating the rights and freedoms of its citizens, and that these are enshrined somewhere for all to see. We have some similar codifications of our own.

The United Nations Universal Declaration on Human Rights

"Human rights include the right to life and liberty, freedom from slavery and torture, freedom of opinion and expression, the right to work and education, and many more. Everyone is entitled to these rights, without discrimination."

The UN specifies 30 basic human rights:

- All human beings are free and equal
- No discrimination
- Right to life
- No slavery
- No torture and inhuman treatment
- Same right to use law
- Equal before the law

- Right to treated fair by court
- No unfair detainment
- Right to trial
- Innocent until proved guilty
- Right to privacy
- Freedom to movement and residence
- Right to asylum
- Right to nationality
- Rights to marry and have family
- Right to own things
- Freedom of thought and religion
- Freedom of opinion and expression
- Right to democracy
- Right to social security
- Right to work
- Right to rest and holiday
- Right of social service
- Right to education
- Right of cultural and art
- Freedom around the world
- Subject to law
- Human rights can't be taken away

The International Covenant on Economic, Social, and Cultural Rights (1976)

The rights that the Covenant seeks to protect include:

- the right to work in just and favorable conditions;
- the right to social protection, to an adequate standard of living and to the highest attainable standards of physical and mental well-being;
- the right to education and the enjoyment of benefits of cultural freedom and scientific progress.

Freedom House

"Democracy depends on the guarantee of equal rights under law and freedom from discrimination for all individuals in a society. If the rights and freedoms of one segment of the population are violated with impunity, the same sorts of abuses are likely to be visited on others. Those forced to endure a subordinate status have less incentive to play by the rules, creating a vicious circle of defiance and repression."

"I'm the President of the United States, not the President of people who agree with me."

Working for the Greater Good

The West Wing frames up the 'greater good' in humble terms, focusing more on the bedrock of social cooperation and mutual support between members of the community than upon sacrificial life-or-death gestures. The Bartlet senior staff understands that the good of the nation is ultimately everyone's highest priority; no one member is more important than any other, and all are committed to the greater good.

This mindset stands in opposition to the Authoritarian's partisanism and bigotry, which cynically projects that each person is in it for themselves, first and foremost, and getting ahead of everyone else is the priority. This was especially true in the entertainment industry, where competition is everything and climbing to the top on the backs of others is commonplace.

Put another way, the *The West Wing* ethos is essentially anti-capitalist. And Sorkin had no problem being very blunt about that. The Bartlet Administration undertakes an agenda that supports individuals and organizations pursuing social justice and equality. Though they never use the word *humanism*, this agenda is in fact very humanist – people first.

The Greater Good

That mindset is a humanist mindset, through-and-through. Though it would be unfair to label the institution of humanism as anti-capitalist, it is certainly fair to say that the humanist views the greater good as a higher priority than personal wealth or success. The humanist is, by definition, on the side of humanity as a whole, rather than in competition with it.

"Humanism is a progressive philosophy of life that, without theism and other supernaturalism, affirms our ability and responsibility to lead ethical lives of personal fulfillment that aspire to the greater good of humanity," says the *Humanist Manifesto III* (2003).

"Humanists are everyday people who espouse the principles of humanism," according to the Humanist Society. "The principles of humanism include helping others, concern for our environment, meeting in community with others of like mind, making connections and growing by connection with others who hold diverse beliefs, and building a legacy that makes our world a better place."

Audrey Kingstrom, president of Humanists of Minnesota, said it like this:

"Unless one can believe in human agency. Own it. Claim it. Not just for oneself, but collectively for the greater good. That's what we must do as a humanist community. Ours is not merely a philosophy on paper. It's a lived experience. Of being our best selves. Living our best lives. And doing the most good that we can in the world. Spreading and sharing the world's good fortune that has graced our own lives.

"As humanists, we don't own the admonition to do good in the world. But we aren't doing it to save anyone's soul or to insure our own reward of heaven. We do it to ease suffering, to bring joy to another, to show compassion, to provide comfort. We do it because we can, because of our own good fortune –

not out of fear or favor.

"We do it to spread a culture of goodness in the world because we know that even if we do not need it now for ourselves, a time will come when we will need it from others. We do it because we understand human frailty and connection. We do it because that is the kind of world we want to live in. One filled with kindness and compassion, civility, and equity. We do it because actions speak louder than words.

"Our good work together as humanists is essential if we are to make our mark on the world. Our service in the community and our advocacy in the public square matters. There is no justice and no goodness other than what we ourselves commit to each other and the world. That's humanism."

Pursuit of the Greater Good

An advantage humanism in practice can claim over other, similar good-of-all philosophies is its emphasis on that agency Kingstrom refers to above. There's a plan of action; there's an implicit requirement that comes with membership, a commitment to make the well-being of others and one's own actions a contribution to the general good that defines the humanist.

"Humanists are clear and certain that the social good, both in the present and future, should be the supreme ethical goal," writes Corliss Lamont in *The Philosophy of Humanism*. "That goal is inclusive of all humanity and envisages the on-going survival of the human race as inherently worthwhile. Logic alone will not win people's assent to the social good as the paramount aim in life; the desirability of that aim is not something that can be proved like a mathematical proposition. It is a vast ethical *assumption*, as important in its field as the scientific assumption of the Uniformity of Nature. Humanism consciously makes this ethical assumption, tries to persuade people in general to make it, and advocates the kind of education that will lead them to make it. Hence the humanist ethic urges the development of those basic impulses of love, friendliness, and cooperation that impel a person to consider constantly the good of the group and to find personal happiness in working for the happiness of all.

"As I have already pointed out, an individual's loyalty to their larger social good may under certain circumstances cost them their very existence or at least consid3erable suffering. We must frankly admit that a person's uncompromising dedication to the happiness of others may lead to unhappiness on their part. A pure conscience is not in itself sufficient to offset the persecution of governments or the cruelty of tyrants. As Aristotle sensibly observed in *The Nicomachean Ethics*: 'To assert that a person on the rack, or a person plunged in the depth of calamities, is happy is either intentionally or unintentionally to talk nonsense.' 'Virtue is its own reward' in the sense that the awareness of doing right always brings spiritual satisfaction; but such satisfaction is not sufficient to make the total person happy when they are suffering excruciating physical punishment. And if they are executed for their virtue, their 'reward' quickly comes to an end altogether.

"On the whole, however, a society in which most individuals, regardless of the personal sacrifices that may be entailed, are devoted to the collective well-being, will attain greater happiness and make more progress than one in which private self-interest and advancement are the prime motivation."

Lamont's framing here is eloquent, and noteworthy for its frankness; he does not shy away from the downside of self-subordination, and is honest about the possible consequences of sacrifice for the greater good.

He also does us the service, in *The Philosophy of Humanism*, of outlining why a society built upon such a principle will do better than others:

- A society made up of cooperative, socially-conscious individuals will be more a society of progress and achievement than one that isn't - and will be happier in the bargain;
- Cooperative society is more fulfilling to human nature, which is inherently gregarious; people are social beings, and our social separations are artificial, not natural; people tend to experience their deepest joys with others, not in solitude;
- Allegiance to the greater good inspires individuals to reach beyond themselves, to pursue wider interests; such efforts, driven by loyalty to one's family and neighbors, imparts stability and harmony, as well as cultivating empathy and a genuine feeling of happiness in the accomplishments of others.

Lamont presents a strong case, and most humanists would affirm both his reasoning and his sentiment. And we can also feel echoes of his argument in our observations on *The West Wing*.

Do We Naturally Seek the Greater Good?

Lamont argues above that the greater good isn't just preferable, it's innate – built into human beings. Is he right?

In his book *Why We Cooperate*, developmental psychologist Michael Tomasello addresses the following question: is cooperation between human beings a naturally emergent behavior or a learned one?

Either way, it's great that it exists, but the implications for our thesis are profound: if the former, then we have within us what we need to achieve a fully humanist future; if the latter, then it will be a far greater struggle, getting where we want to be.

Tomasello begins by pointing to research demonstrating

that infants as young as 18 months overwhelmingly attempt to assist adults whose hands are full. He cites this as one of five reasons to believe that this cooperative impulse in very small children is a naturally emergent human trait. It's the first of five:

1. Very small children impulsively help others without prompting or training;
2. Parental reward does not alter the outcome of #1; the child will impulsively help with or without reward;
3. Chimpanzee infants exhibit the same behaviors;
4. Human children exhibit the behavior across a diverse range of cultures;
5. Experiments have shown that helping behavior in young children is mediated by empathy – they will tend to help an adult they perceive to be a victim before helping another.

Tomasello continues to methodically develop a portrait of cooperation as evolutionary, building toward this conclusion: "...the changes we see in human societies beginning with the advent of agriculture and cities are not due, on anyone's account, to any kind of biological adaptation," he wrote. "The changes would seem to be sociological only, given their recency and the fact that by this time modern humans were already spread out all over the glove (so that a species-wide biological change was highly unlikely). What this means is that most, if not all, of the highly complex forms of cooperation in modern industrial societies – from the United Nations to credit card purchases over the Internet – are built primarily on cooperative skills ant motivations biologically evolved for small-group interactions: the kinds of altruistic and collaborative activities that we have seen here in our simple studies of great apes and young children."

We have good reason to believe, then, that the deep

cooperation that binds humanity doesn't need to be contrived; it just needs to be awakened.

Lost

Genetic variety in both our ancient (limbic) and modern (cortical) brain components – those contributing to social reasoning, in particular – gives us a group of distinct cognitive "types," each with different cognitive strengths and decision-making style. No one human mind can encompass the variety expressed by this range of distinct types; it takes a group of humans – a diverse group, with many persons of each type – fully express the potential of human reason and decision-making. And that potential, by evolution's hand, is how humankind has managed to meet the needs of the many, since our beginnings.

The problem is... we've lost our way. Our modern social organization robs of us the value of the cognitive diversity that we absolutely will need to meet the challenges that threaten us, both today and tomorrow.

The greater good – the needs of the many – is clearly the guiding light of the American future, as visualized by *The West Wing*. The Bartlet Administration's liberal vision is a world where poverty and oppression have been vanquished, where everyone enjoys sustenance and dignity and opportunity – a world that can only happen when the greater good is the highest social priority, above wealth and power and status. It's that vision, a future defined by a moral clarity and ethical maturity far beyond what we've achieved so far, that draws many to the Sorkin mythos: they want to live in a *West Wing* future.

And that's the future a successful resistance can bring.

"I really like him, Leo. I want to hire him."
"What's the problem?"
"He's black."
"So's the Attorney General and the Chairman of the Joint Chiefs."

Diversity

Few attributes of the *West Wing* universe stand out as starkly as its commitment to diversity. There are lots of white guys, sure, but the roster of women in power is substantial; the number of characters in positions of authority who are black or otherwise members of ethnic minorities is likewise very high.

And they are not just token presences. Charlie Young isn't just a black man holding the door for a white president; he's openly portrayed as the smartest guy in whatever room he's in. Abbey Bartlet is no ceremonial First Lady; she's a brilliant scientist, an accomplished surgeon. Admiral Fitzwallace is shown to be utterly expert in his role; Amy Gardner is fiercely competent, a match for even as devious an opponent as Josh.

That commitment would continue throughout the series, until a woman ascends to Chief of Staff, another becomes Chief Justice of the Supreme Court, and a Latino becomes President Bartlet's successor.

These examples (and there are, of course, many more) project an image of an administration that has embraced diversity across the spectrum, unburdened by the racism, ethnocentrism, misogyny and other social toxins that still contaminate American politics in the real world.

It is exactly this commitment to diversity, and the recognition that its absence is toxic to us all, that motivates those who would resist the Authoritarian, to whom diversity is anathema. It is an integral part of the liberal social framework, and tops the list of liberal aspirations for America's progress.

Otherness vs. Sameness

The health and benefit of diversity might seem so obvious and essential that it might baffle those who embrace it that anyone would feel otherwise. But, of course, many do; on the flip side of diversity we find xenophobia – more recently rebranded *othering*, the ancient tradition of lumping some people into a rejected or despised group apart from one's own.

Othering serves up mirror-image versions of diversity's categories: there is ethnic othering, religious othering, gender- or sex-based othering. Political othering, in particular, has made a spectacle of itself in recent years.

What is at the core of othering?

"Othering is not about liking or disliking someone," wrote John A. Powell in *The Guardian*. "It is based on the conscious or unconscious assumption that a certain identified group poses a threat to the favoured group. It is largely driven by politicians and the media, as opposed to personal contact. Overwhelmingly, people don't "know" those that they are

Othering."

It's that threat that drives otherness, wrote Čega se bojiš on Wordpress. "The fear of otherness is closely linked to the fear of the unknown and to the degree of trust in people. It is based on the fact that someone by their existence endangers what we consider 'our own' or 'ours.' It is often manifested in the form of fear that someone who has a different cultural characteristic to us – such as faith, language, customs and value system – endangers 'our' culture and way of life. According to this matrix, the influx of other people's elements into our cultural register leads to the long-term loss of 'our' identity and cultural affiliation.

"Otherness does not often come from far away. It is found in the neighbourhood, partly in the society and community to which we belong. Someone from a rival fan camp, someone on an opposing political-ideological spectrum, someone of extremely different material possibilities or understanding of sexual orientation and gender affiliation is a representative of the otherness which in the most radical forms often becomes a source of collective and individual fears."

In a 2016 interview by Jeffrey Goldberg in *The Atlantic*, then-President Barack Obama cited othering as the primary source of most of the world's conflict: "tribe - us/them, a hostility toward the unfamiliar or unknown." It's not hard to see this reality reflected in even a cursory reading of human history; anywhere diversity has been lacking, othering has flourished, to the detriment at all.

Liberals, whose focus is persistently fixed on a positive human future, understandably see othering as a significant barrier to be addressed in progressing toward that future. The embrace and tireless nourishing of diversity everywhere is essential to tearing down that barrier.

Ancient Human Diversity

But diversity is more than a key to future harmony and growth. Diversity was, ironically, the key to human survival, when we were genetically at our most Homogenous.

Confined in our earlier millennia to Central Africa, we had not yet developed the broad range of skin tones we now enjoy; our culture in particular was decidedly monotone, as we had not yet developed writing, art, or even language.

Yet we had already begun experiencing the most important diversity of all: differences in thought.

By this, we aren't thinking of differences in philosophies or doctrines or ideologies like those that surround us today – those things didn't yet exist. We're talking about *literal* differences in thought – the actual variations that existed (and still exist!) in human brains, diversity in proportional quantities of brain tissue in different brain regions – diversity that resulted (and still does today) in some variation in how each of us processes the world.

We've looked at those brain variations themselves, and how different combinations of brain components resulted in different cognitive contributions to tribal survival. And we've considered how destructive it is when that cognitive diversity is dampened when humans cluster together in cults of like-mindedness. Now let's look at the evidence.

Diversity Makes Us Smarter

"Great things in business are never done by one person. They're done by a team of people."

~Steve Jobs

Scientific American gathered together summaries of a number of studies demonstrating the advantages of diversity in the workplace,[44] concluding that being around people who think differently increases our creativity and diligence.

Cristian Deszö of the University of Maryland and David Ross of Columbia University, for instance, noted the impact of gender diversity in business. Reviewing the size and gender make-up of the top equity firms from 1992-2006, they found that, on average, firms with women in top management positions demonstrated greater financial performance than those without. Orlando Richard of the University of Texas found in a 2003 study that the same holds true for racial diversity in upper management.

A 2006 study at the University of Illinois teamed subjects to solve a murder mystery exercise, varying the racial make-up of the three-person teams. Teams with a non-white member significantly out-performed all-white teams.

Another University of Illinois study in 2013 tasked subjects to identify as either Democrat or Republican, then read a murder mystery and decide who they thought committed the crime.

They were then tasked to write an essay making their case, for presentation to another test subject in hopes of convincing them. Half of the subjects were told they would be making the case to a member of their own political party; half were told they'd be trying to convince a member of the other party. Subjects of both parties prepared less well and wrote a less persuasive essay when they believed they were going to be talking to a member of their own party. "Diversity jolts us into cognitive action in ways that Homogeneity simply does not," the study concluded.

And in 2014, Richard Freeman and Wei Huang of Harvard University examined ethnicity among the authors of 1.5 million scientific papers, noting that those written by ethnically

---

diverse research teams received more citations than those written by teams of people with common ethnicity.

Finally there's a 2006 study by Samuel Sommers of Tufts University, where real judges, jury administrators and jurors participated in a mock jury experiment to determine the effects of racial diversity in jury decision-making. Sommers arranged the jurors into all-white groups and four-white, two-black groups. The diverse juries made fewer errors in recall of important information and discussed the role of race in the case more openly. Sommers concluded that in the presence of diversity, white jurors "were more diligent and open-minded," according to *Scientific American*.

Cognitive diversity and performance

But gender, race, and political orientation, though qualifying as diversity, do not necessarily imply *cognitive* diversity. In an article in the *Harvard Business Review*, Alison Reynolds and David Lewis took up the problem, using Peter Robertson's AEM Cube tool to assess a person's knowledge processing and perspective in new situations.

Six teams were created, variable in their degree of AEM Cube ratings, and were then given a group task to complete. The teams with greater diversity in knowledge processing and perspective completed the exercise more quickly; the greater the level of diversity, the higher the team's score.

Reynolds and Lewis further noted that cognitive diversity is a more reliable performance enhancer than gender and racial diversity, comparing the AEM Cube study to other performance studies:

"Someone being from a different culture or a different generation gives no clue as to how that person might process information, engage with, or respond to change," they wrote. "We cannot easily detect cognitive diversity from the outside. It cannot be predicted or easily orchestrated. The very fact that it is an internal difference requires us to work hard to surface it and harness the benefits."

"We were no longer subjects of King George III, but rather a self-governing people."

The Essence of Democracy

"My great-grandfather's great-grandfather was Dr. Josiah Bartlet," the President tells an auditorium full of students in Rosslyn, "who was the New Hampshire delegate to the Second Continental Congress, the one that sat in session in Philadelphia in the summer of 1776 and announced to the world that we were no longer subjects of King George III, but rather a self-governing people. 'We hold these truths to be self-evident,' they said, 'that all men are created equal.' Strange as it may seem, that was the first time in history that anyone had bothered to write that down."[45]

The actual story of human democracy – egalitarian self-governance within a social group – is more complex than we generally learn while growing up, and at the same time more

---

[45] In "What Kind of Day Has It Been?", S1/E22.

universal than we've been led to believe.

It's more complex in that the great American Experiment that commenced in the 18th century is often portrayed as a reflection of the Roman Republic, in form, and a product of the French Enlightenment, in philosophy. The form – representative government of all citizens – was a loose match, but fair enough; the philosophy – that human beings, living in a democratic order, are at their natural best – was a much stronger match, heavily derivative of the work of John Locke and Jean-Jacques Rousseau.

The thing is – though many of us were brought up with this basic understanding of where modern democracy originated, Roman Republic to the French Enlightenment to America's Framers – that's just the bare bones of the actual story.

From Rome to Britain to France

Thom Hartmann provides a deeper take in his book *The Hidden History of American Democracy*. Yes, he writes, Ben Franklin and John Adams and Thomas Jefferson all went to Europe and picked up a lot of Enlightenment thought – and, yes, they were well versed in the political philosophy of the Roman Republic – but where did the French philosophers get *their* inspiration?

It turns out that inspiration came full circle: they got it from *the social order of the Native Americans.*

Hartmann notes that the thinkers of the Enlightenment were at first replying, in no small measure, to the 17th century writings of Thomas Hobbes, a British philosopher who posited that the natural human was a brutish, savage creature, only tamed through the use of political and social force. In his book *Leviathan*, Hobbes took the stance that only a powerful autocratic state or rigidly enforced religion was capable of bringing order to humankind; without it, anarchy would inevitably prevail. After all, wasn't such a structure to be seen in all nation-states, back to the beginning of civilization? Aren't *all* societies ruled by powerful, wealthy kings or rigid priesthoods?

Over the next century, a new generation of philosophers recoiled from that ghastly vision. Hobbes's countryman John Locke, in his *Two Treatises of Government* and *An Essay Concerning Human Understanding*, argued that the former's cynical take on human nature, however biblical it might be, was far off the mark; human beings, Locke suggested, are *not* born evil, are *not* naturally violent and selfish, and do *not* require dominant men of power and wealth to create a successful social order.

Locke had a millennium of European history working against him, but was undeterred; the truth of human nature was true irrespective of how long it had been apparent, he argued. He proceeded, in the face of much criticism, to suggest that "Man being born, as has been proved, with a title to perfect freedom and an uncontrolled enjoyment of all the rights and privileges of the law of nature, equally with any other man, or number of men in the world, hath by nature a power, not only to preserve his property, that is, life, liberty, and estate, against the injuries and attempts of other men."

He went on to write that "Nature, I confess, has put into man a desire of happiness and an aversion to misery: these indeed are innate practical principles."

These two statements, Hartmann points out, were synthesized by Thomas Jefferson in the Declaration of Independence.

Later came Jean-Jacques Rousseau, who connected the benign natural state of humanity advanced by Locke into a political form, suggesting (per Hartmann) that "the laws of nature were essentially democratic and noble and that the closer humanity could come to following natural law, the closer we'd be to a life of freedom and happiness."

Hartmann goes on to quote Rousseau: "There you see how luxury, dissolution, and slavery have in every age been the punishment for the arrogant efforts we have made in order to emerge from the happy ignorance where Eternal Wisdom had placed us."

Rousseau was adding the touch that wealth, power and social dominance didn't seem to have a place in Nature's Eternal Wisdom or Happy Ignorance. This, the Framers synthesized with Locke's assertion that while "divine law" placed men in authority over other men, Nature's law was based on their approval of their governors: a government was only legitimate if it derived that legitimacy from the "consent of the governed."

That's a powerful idea, and if we left it at that, we'd still have a narrative that was coherent and functional. But there are, Hartmann says, two additional layers.

Beyond the Human Being

Suppose Locke was right, and Nature's laws favored democratic community? Wouldn't this necessarily extend beyond humankind? After all, there are other social animals on the planet.

Hartmann points out that science has, in recent years, confirmed that this is indeed the case:[46]

"In the first paragraph of the Declaration of Independence, Jefferson wrote that 'the laws of nature and of nature's God' compelled America's Founders to reject British oligarchy and embrace democracy," Hartmann wrote. "But was he right? Is nature actually democratic? Biologists Tim Roper and L. Conradt at the School of Life Sciences, University of Sussex, England, studied this issue in animals.

"We've always assumed that the alpha or leader animal of the herd or group makes the decision, and the others follow,

---

[46] In Hartmann's *The Hidden History of American Oligarchy*, pp. 52-54.

like the human kings and queens of old. The leader knows best, we believe: he or she is prepared for that genetically by generations of Darwinian natural selection.

"But it turns out there's a system for voting among animals, from honeybees to primates, that we've just never noticed because we weren't looking for it. 'Many authors have assumed despotism without testing [for democracy],' Conradt and Roper wrote in a *Nature* article about the study, 'because the feasibility of democracy, which requires the ability to vote and to count votes, is not immediately obvious in non-humans.' Stepping into this vacuum of knowledge, the two scientists decided to create a testable model that 'compares the synchronization costs of despotic and democratic groups.'

"Conradt and Roper discovered that when a single leader (what they call a despot) or a small group of leaders (the animal equivalent of an oligarchy) makes the choices, the swings into extremes of behavior tend to be greater and more dangerous to the long-term survival of the group. Because in a despotic model the overall needs of the entire group are measured only by the leader's needs, wrong decisions would be made often enough to put the survival of the group at risk. With democratic decision-making, however, the overall knowledge and wisdom of the entire group, as well as the needs of the entire group, come into play. The outcome is less likely to harm anybody, and the group's probability of survival is enhanced. 'Democratic decisions are more beneficial primarily because they tend to produce less extreme decisions,' they noted in the abstract to their paper.

"Britain's leading mass-circulation science journal, *New Scientist*, looked at how Conradt and Roper's model played out in the natural world. They examined the behavior of a herd of red deer, which are social animals with alpha leaders. What they found was startling: Red deer always behave democratically. When more than half of the animals were pointing at a particular watering hole, for example, the entire group would then move in that direction. 'In the case of real red deer,' James Randerson noted, 'the animals do indeed vote with their feet by standing up. Likewise, with groups of African buffalo, individuals decide where to go by pointing in their preferred direction. The group takes the average and heads that way.' This explains in part the flock, swarm, and school nature of birds, gnats, and fish. With each wingbeat or fin motion, each member is 'voting' for the direction in which the flock, swarm, or school should move; when the 51 percent threshold is hit, the entire group moves as if telepathically synchronized.

"Tim Roper told me, 'Quite a lot of people have said, 'My gorillas do that,' or 'My animals do that.' On an informal, anecdotal basis, it [the article] seems to have triggered an 'Oh, yes, that's quite true' reaction in field workers.' I asked him if his theory that animals - and, by inference, humans in their 'natural state' - operate democratically contradicted Darwin. He was emphatic. 'I don't think it is [at variance with Darwin]... So the point about this model is that democratic decision-making is best for all the individuals in the group, as opposed to following a leader, a dominant individual. So we see it as an individual selection model, and so it's not incompatible with Darwin at all.' Democracy, it turns out, is the norm in the animal kingdom, for the simple reason that it confers the greatest likelihood that the group will survive and prosper."

The Indigenous Critique

More than a few voices in paleontology and anthropology have suggested that Paleolithic humans were not at all savage and did not practice social dominance, but were instead egalitarian in their social order and equality-minded in their economics – owing, more than anything, to their lack of the concept of "property" or "wealth". What happened to one, happened to all; the members of any given human tribe were all in it together.

Civilization, originating in the Fertile Crescent and spreading throughout the Middle East in all directions, put an end to that. Agriculture, for all its power to feed more people and make possible the long-term storage of food – surplus – also bestowed the concepts of property and wealth, ownership, and stratified society. It was a very mixed blessing.

And when civilized humans began crossing the oceans and made their way to the Americas, they were closing that circle: humans who had lived through 200 generations of civilization, with its kings and armies and religions and treasures and poverty and slavery and genocides, found themselves face-to-face with humans who were *still in their Edenic state* – latter-day Paleoliths, still living according to Nature's laws, unsullied by wealth and property and class and autocracy.

Those humans included the Wendat, better known to history as the Huron tribe of the Iroquois Confederacy, encountered by French Jesuit missionaries who had hiked into Canada to save their souls. They were astonished by what they found.

"I do not believe there is any people on earth freer than they, and less able to allow the subjection of their wills to any power whatever," wrote Father Lallemant in *Jesuit Relations* in 1644, "so much so that Fathers here have no control over their children, or Captains over their subjects, or the Laws of the Country over any of them, except in so far as each is pleased to submit to them. There is no punishment which is inflicted on the guilty, and no criminal who is not sure that his life and property are in no danger."

How did the Wendat achieve this? "Consent of the governed" – the principle that would makes its way to Thomas Jefferson by way of Locke and Rousseau.

Governance among the Wendat was achieved Bartlet-style: through dialog and debate – smart people disagreeing.

"When the governed agreed, decisions were made or punishments meted out," Hartmann writes. "When they didn't, things were worked out in dialogue and debate, sometimes lasting days."

"This form of justice restrains all of these peoples, and seems more effectually to repress disorders than the personal punishment of criminals does in France," Lallemant wrote.

These writings took Europe by storm, triggering an insatiable curiosity about Native Americans that persisted for decades.

"I can say in truth that, as regards intelligence, they are in no wise inferior to Europeans and to those who dwell in France. I would never have believed that, without instruction, nature could have supplied a most ready and vigorous eloquence, which I have admired in many Hurons; or more clear-sightedness in public affairs, or a more discreet management in things to which they are accustomed."

The Baron De Lahontan, a Dutchman, would write, half a century later, of his dialogs with "an unusually brilliant Wendat statesman named Kandiaronk." His writings took up where the Jesuits had left off, giving Europe another look into the lives of humans still in Nature's arms, untouched by the afflictions of civilization. Ben Franklin was busy being born as those writings spread across Europe like wildfire, going through a dozen reprintings in a wide array of languages – and setting in motion the pens of the Enlightenment philosophers in Britain and France.

De Lahontan's dialog with his Wendat companion surfaced many criticisms of European society, overall a scathing indictment. Lahontan described Native America's own social order with astonishment:

"They think it unaccountable that one man should have more than another, and that the rich should have more respect than the poor. In short, they say, the name of 'savages', which we bestow upon them, would fit ourselves better, since there is nothing in our actions that bears an appearance of wisdom."

A 19-year-old Thomas Jefferson would meet such a Native American leader face to face – the Cherokee diplomat

Ontasseté, who spent a great deal of time in colonial cities and towns, and would travel to England to negotiate a treaty with King George II. He and his brother Framers were very clear on the concepts by which these out-of-time people lived, how they managed their society. And it was on those ideas that they built the first true democracy in the civilized world.

We face the rise of the Authoritarian in the West today because we haven't gone far enough in the direction of either the Native America of the past or the Bartlet vision of the future. One of our *West Wing*-inspired commitments must be, not only to the principle of governance by the consent of the governed, but the uncompromising practice of universal social and economic equality among the governed.

"There are times when we're 50 states, and there are times when we're one country, and have national needs."

On the Other Side of Resistance

Again, *The West Wing*'s liberalism holds much in common with humanism – including a vision that extends beyond America to the world in general. It was in that spirit of global unity that the Bartlet Doctrine was born in "Inauguration: Over There" (S4/E15) – a determination that the US would intervene, with military strength if necessary, for purely humanitarian purposes.

That determination to support human well-being across the social spectrum and beyond American borders is increasingly important to the liberal agenda – and has been part of the humanist agenda all along.

"Perhaps the most exciting fact of modern humanism is that its world is becoming genuinely global and that it is viscerally and ideologically prepared for that fact," wrote Howard Radest, senior fellow at the Institute for Humanist Studies, in Anthony Pinn's *What is Humanism and Why Does It Matter?* "Humanist universalism is matched for the first time in history by geopolitical and cultural realities."

Globalization, and the human interconnectedness of the Internet in particular, are nudging humanity in a humanist direction, according to Krysia Gayle Solon, a scholar of the Humanist Alliance Philippines International.

"As the world has grown closer to each other because of globalization, so too has humanity," she said. "Humans have grown more trusting of one another rather than praying to the divines for answers or material objects. Instead of placing their trust solely in divine entities, many humans now rely on the wonders of science and prioritize progress for the good of mankind. Humanity has grown to be there for one another not because it was through the will of the divines, but because we have learned to be more thoughtful of others.

"This is Humanism, the act of placing more importance on other human beings rather than the divines. It encourages the people to utilize technological advancements, scientific discoveries, and innovations to ensure a bright future for the succeeding generations to come."

Charles Taylor, in his book *A Secular Age*, posits the nova effect: "...an ever-widening variety of moral/spiritual options, across the span of the thinkable and perhaps even beyond." Tone Svetelj of Boston College advances the idea that Taylor's nova effect is itself unifying in the paper "Universal Humanism – A Globalization Context is the Classroom of Unheard Options... how to Become More Human":

"...the humanism that includes all people and nations – for this reason I call it a universal humanism – allows us to discover in a new perspective what is universally human by transcending our spatial and temporal frames.

"Universal humanism permits us who live in modern Western societies to be at the deepest level of our existence in touch with commonalities among other human agents from the present and past times, both in and outside of Western societies. This humanism commits us to respect all specific definitions of humanism (Greek, Roman, German, Italian, Romantic, Christian, Muslim, Buddhist, exclusive, inclusive, and similar) on the one side, and on the other, challenges us to transcend them all and integrate each one of them into something what would be even more meaningful."

The Welsh writer Mick Antoniw makes the argument that the solutions to the specific problems that globalization is tugging into high relief are all contained within humanism:

"We live in a world where it is predicted that by 2030 50% of the world's wealth will be in the hands of 1% of the population. Half the world flourishes whilst half the world starves.

"As inequality increases, societies become increasingly unstable, growing nationalisms set people against people, barriers are erected and the seeds of conflict are sown.

"Humanism as with ethical socialism is about the belief that the power to resolve all these problems lies in our hands, through our rational analysis, through the use of science for the benefit of all through a recognition or our common humanity and obligations to one another."

Mike Whitty, a scholar for Global Citizens for Tolerance and Decency, sees globalization in its current state as fanning culture wars both within and between nations. He proposes humanism as a solution to that problem:

"Global humanism is an antidote to human alienation and fear thus the importance of outreach organizing to re-balance future evolution toward a future of tolerance and acceptance of our unity in diversity.

"Tolerance, civility and non-violence are the first steps toward a truce in the cultural wars. This truce buys time and allows freedom and liberty to grow in the hearts and minds of youth.

"Most thought leaders, especially tomorrow's youth, see the necessity of a live-and-let-live future, and acceptance of our circumstances until humanity evolves to a new paradigm of global humanism."

And, finally, the very reliable philosopher Bertrand Russell addresses the question of the future, putting a humanist spin on his most optimistic option, in his essay "The Future of Mankind":[47]

"Before the end of the present century, unless something quite unforeseeable occurs, one of three possibilities will have been realized. These three are:

- The end of human life, perhaps of all life on our planet.
- A reversion to barbarism after a catastrophic diminution of the population of the globe.
- A unification of the world under a single government, possessing a monopoly of all the major weapons of war.

"I do not pretend to know which of these will happen, or even which is the most likely. What I do contend is that the kind of system to which we have been accustomed cannot possibly continue.

- "The first possibility, the extinction of the human race, is not to be expected in the next world war, unless that war is postponed for a longer time than now seems probable. But if the next world war is indecisive, or if the victors are unwise, and if organized states survive it, a period of feverish technical development may be expected to follow its conclusion. With vastly more powerful means of utilizing atomic energy than those now available, it is thought by many sober men of science that radioactive clouds, drifting round the world, may disintegrate living tissue everywhere. Although the last survivor may proclaim himself universal

---

[47] Reprinted in his collection *Unpopular Essays*.

Emperor, his reign will be brief and his subjects will all be corpses. With his death the uneasy episode of life will end, and the peaceful rocks will revolve unchanged until the sun explodes.

- "The second possibility, that of a reversion to barbarism, would leave open the likelihood of a gradual return to civilization, as after the fall of Rome. The sudden transition will, if it occurs, be infinitely painful to those who experience it, and for some centuries afterwards life will be hard and drab. But at any rate there will still be a future for mankind, and the possibility of rational hope.

"I think such an outcome of a really scientific world war is by no means improbable. Imagine each side in a position to destroy the chief cities and centers of industry of the enemy; imagine an almost complete obliteration of laboratories and libraries, accompanied by a heavy casualty rate among men of science; imagine famine due to radioactive spray, and pestilence caused by bacteriological warfare: Would social cohesion survive such strains? Would not prophets tell the maddened populations that their ills were wholly due to science, and that the extermination of all educated men would bring the millennium? Extreme hopes are born of extreme misery, and in such a world hopes could only be irrational. I think the great states to which we are accustomed would break up, and the sparse survivors would revert to a primitive village economy.

- "The third possibility, that of the establishment of a single government for the whole world, might be realized in various ways: by the victory of the United States in the next world war, or by the victory of the USSR, or, theoretically, by agreement.

Or—and I think this is the most hopeful of the issues that are in any degree probable—by an alliance of the nations that desire an international government, becoming, in the end, so strong that Russia would no longer dare to stand out. This might conceivably be achieved without another world war, but it would require courageous and imaginative statesmanship in a number of countries."

Can we push back the Authoritarian and reinvigorate democracy? Can we achieve the unity to which Bartlet liberalism aspires?

Bertrand Russell felt we really have no choice:

"If we are to live together and not die together, we must learn a kind of charity and a kind of tolerance which is absolutely vital to the continuation of human life on the planet."

Sounds a lot like Jed Bartlet, doesn't he?

"Be as courageous as you can. If none of us is prepared to die for freedom, then all of us will die under tyranny."

~Timothy Snyder

If you enjoyed
What's Next? By Those Who Show Up,
leave a review on Amazon.com!

See more of
the *What's Next?* series
on the following pages...

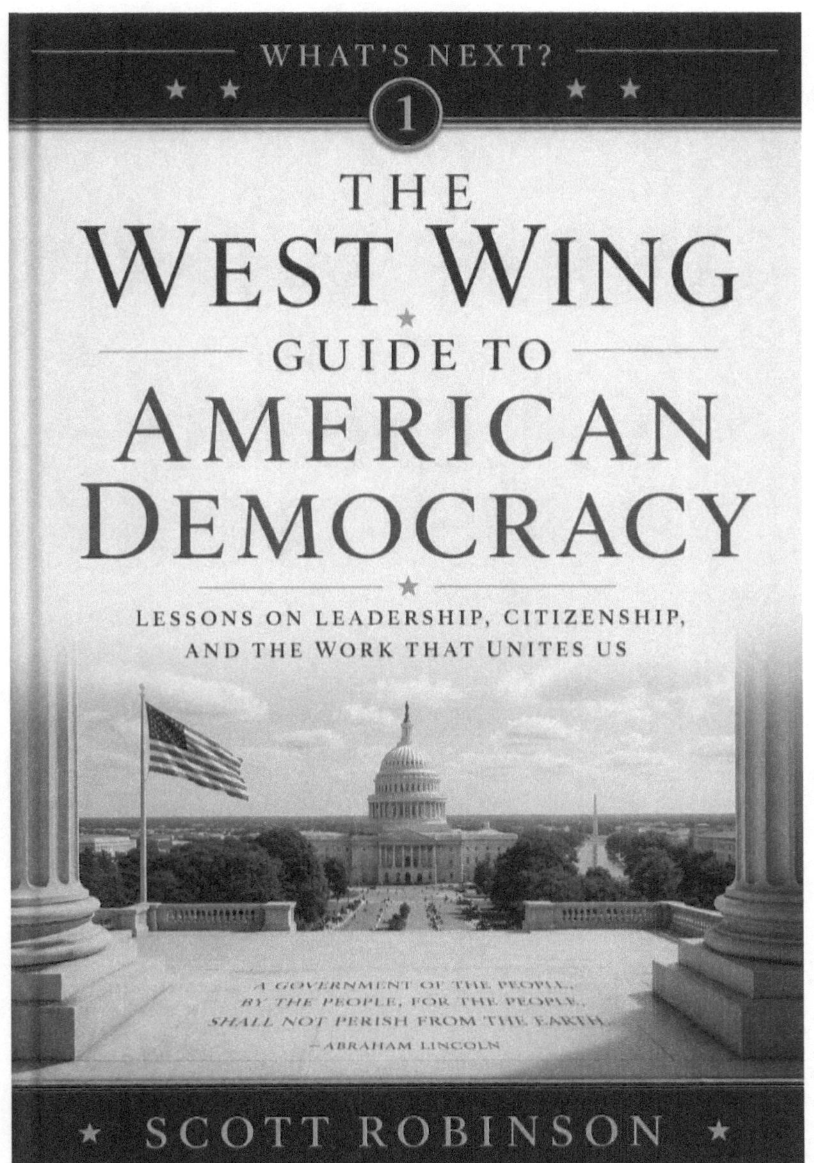
WHAT'S NEXT?
1
THE
WEST WING
GUIDE TO
AMERICAN
DEMOCRACY
LESSONS ON LEADERSHIP, CITIZENSHIP,
AND THE WORK THAT UNITES US
A GOVERNMENT OF THE PEOPLE,
BY THE PEOPLE, FOR THE PEOPLE,
SHALL NOT PERISH FROM THE EARTH.
— ABRAHAM LINCOLN
SCOTT ROBINSON

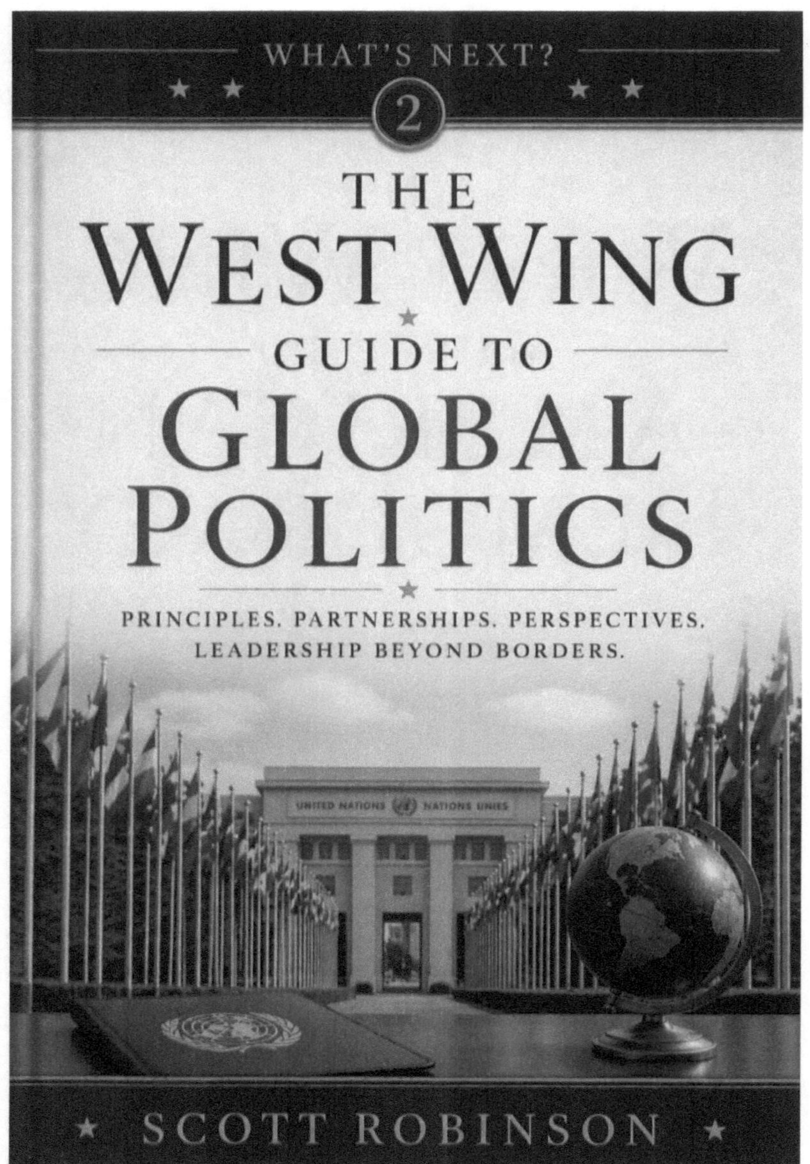
WHAT'S NEXT?
2
THE
WEST WING
GUIDE TO
GLOBAL
POLITICS
PRINCIPLES. PARTNERSHIPS. PERSPECTIVES.
LEADERSHIP BEYOND BORDERS.
UNITED NATIONS NATIONS UNIES
SCOTT ROBINSON

WHAT'S NEXT?
3
THE
WEST WING
ULTIMATE
SUPERFAN
TRIVIA CHALLENGE!
TRIVIA QUIZZES FROM ALL 7 SEASONS
QUESTION:
What vegetable does
President Bartlet dislike?
A. Spinach
B. Cabbage
C. Green Beans
D. Corn
THE
WEST WING
SCOTT ROBINSON

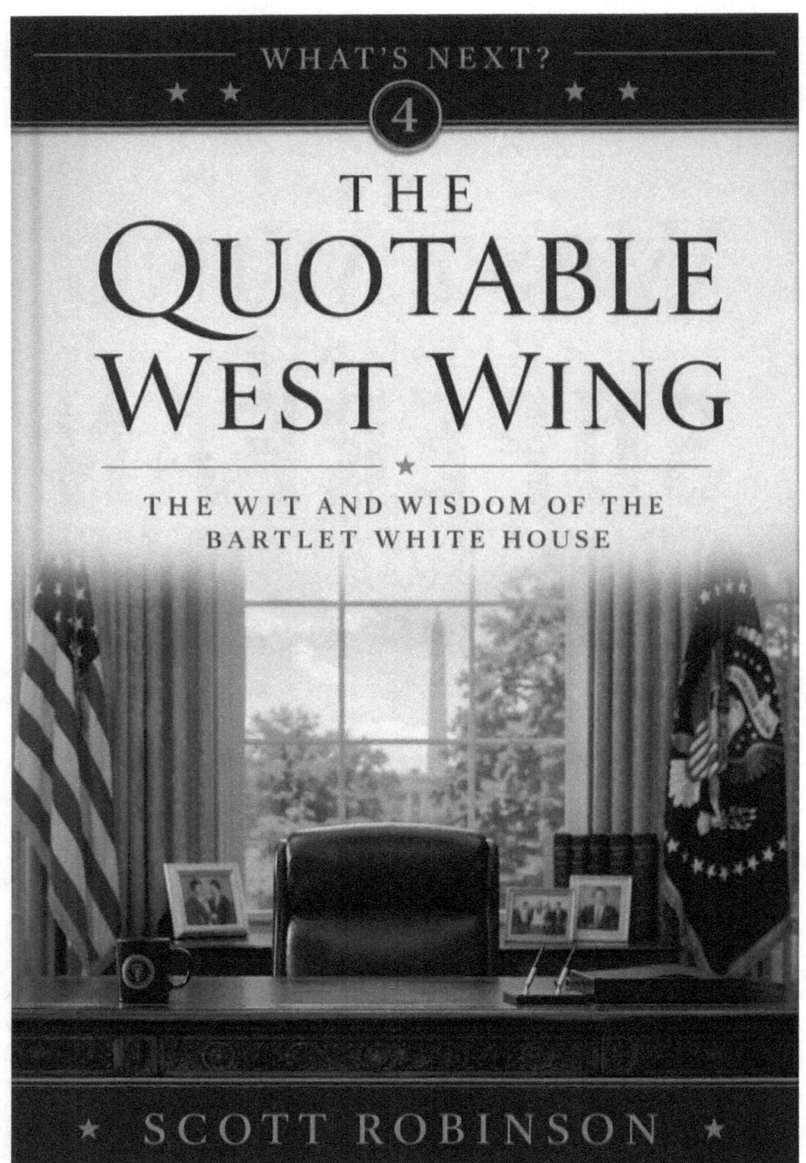

WHAT'S NEXT?
4
THE
QUOTABLE
WEST WING
THE WIT AND WISDOM OF THE
BARTLET WHITE HOUSE
SCOTT ROBINSON

WHAT'S NEXT?
5
THE
WEST WING
BIG BOOK OF
SUPERFAN
FUN!
TRIVIA, STORIES, AND ESSAYS ABOUT
TV'S GREATEST DRAMATIC SERIES!
What's Next?
THE
WEST WING
PRESIDENT
BARTLET
SCOTT ROBINSON

RED BRAINS, BLUE BRAINS
The Psychology of MAGA
Scott Robinson

RED BRAINS,
BLUE BRAINS
Authoritarian We Will Go!
Scott Robinson

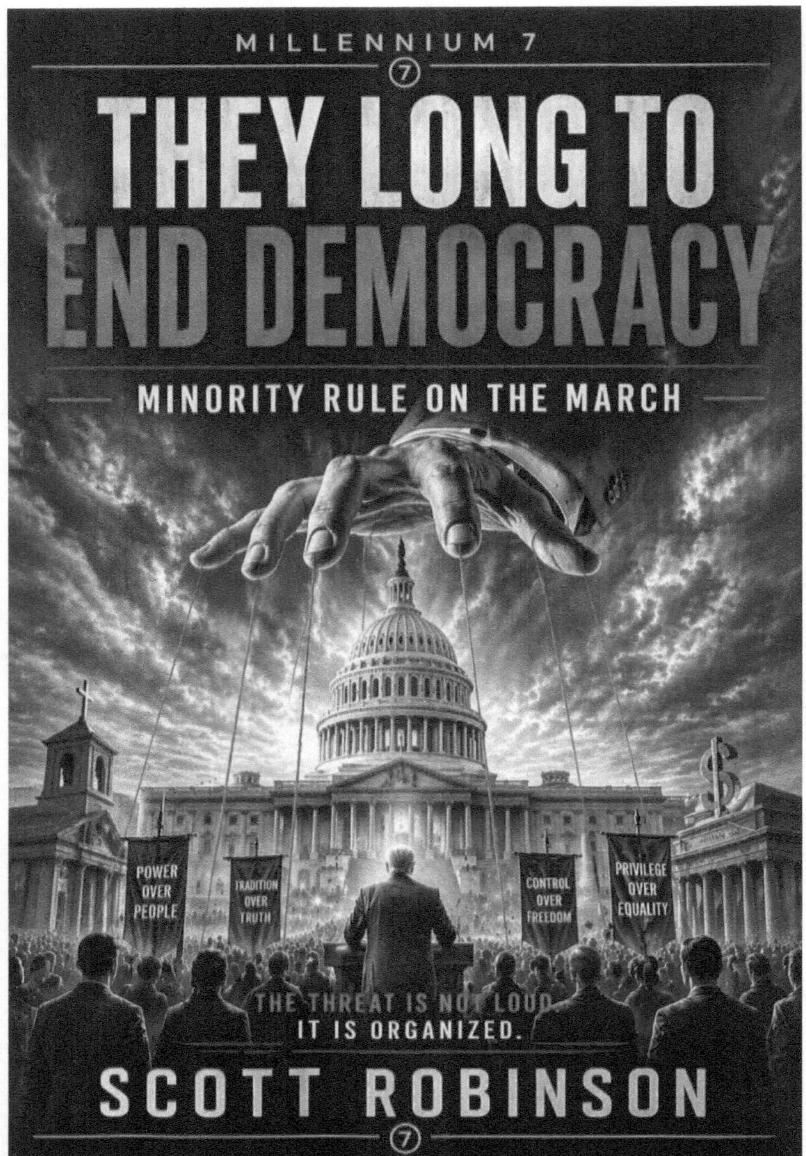
MILLENNIUM 7
7
THEY LONG TO END DEMOCRACY
MINORITY RULE ON THE MARCH
POWER OVER PEOPLE
TRADITION OVER TRUTH
CONTROL OVER FREEDOM
PRIVILEGE OVER EQUALITY
THE THREAT IS NOT LOUD.
IT IS ORGANIZED.
SCOTT ROBINSON
7

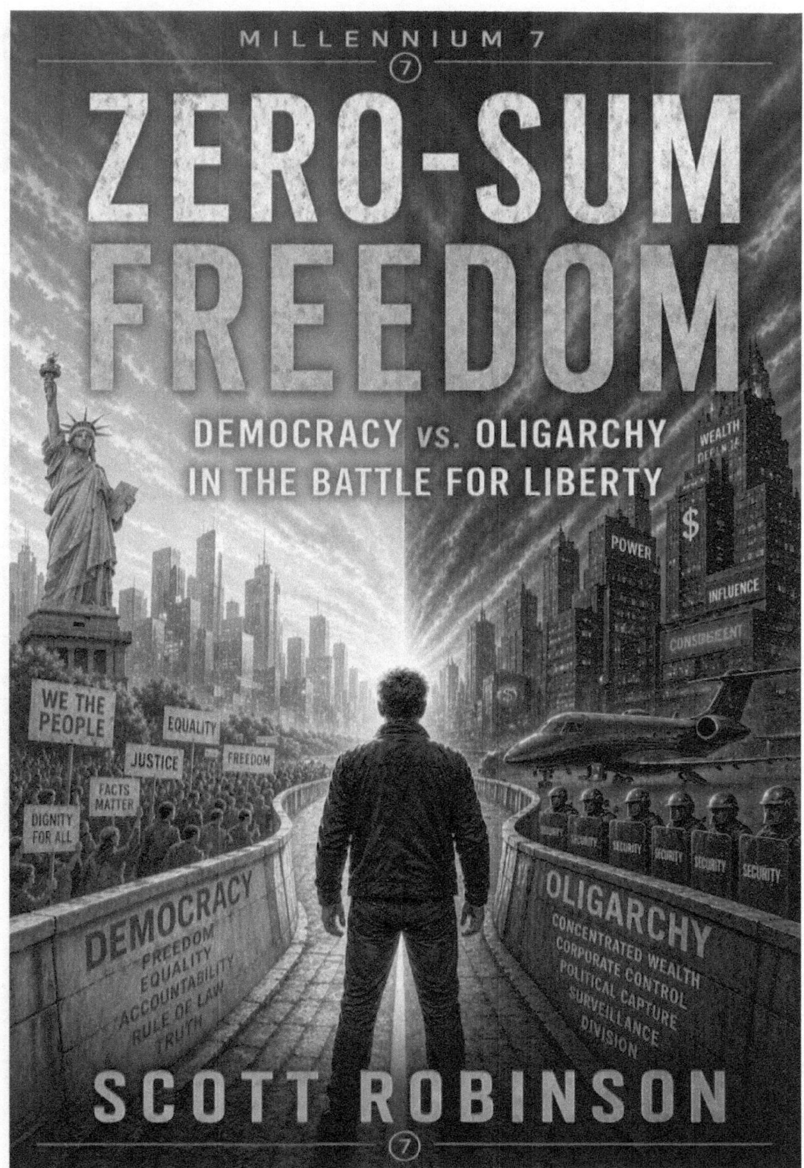

MILLENNIUM 7
7
ZERO-SUM
FREEDOM
DEMOCRACY vs. OLIGARCHY
IN THE BATTLE FOR LIBERTY
WEALTH
$
POWER
INFLUENCE
WE THE PEOPLE
EQUALITY
JUSTICE
FREEDOM
FACTS MATTER
DIGNITY FOR ALL
SECURITY
SECURITY
SECURITY
SECURITY
SECURITY
DEMOCRACY
FREEDOM
EQUALITY
ACCOUNTABILITY
RULE OF LAW
TRUTH
OLIGARCHY
CONCENTRATED WEALTH
CORPORATE CONTROL
POLITICAL CAPTURE
SURVEILLANCE
DIVISION
SCOTT ROBINSON
7

EXPLORING THE ETHICS OF THE FINAL FRONTIER

STAR TREK AND HUMANISM

Living by the Star Trek Ethos in a Troubled World

SCOTT ROBINSON

BOLDLY GOING — BOOK #1

*What would it take to actually build
the world Star Trek imagined?*

PLURIBUS
JOY & DREAD
IN THE BENEVOLENT MACHINE
SCOTT ROBINSON

Bibliography/Recommended Reading

The Authoritarian Specter, Altemeyer, R. Harvard University Press, 1996.

The Authoritarians, Altemeyer, R. Cherry Hill Publishing, 2009.

The Bill of Obligations: The Ten Habits of Good Citizens, Haass, R. Penguin Press, 2023.

Bowling Alone: The Collapse and Revival of American Community, Putman, R. Simon & Schuster, 2001.

Don't Think of an Elephant! Know Your Values and Frame the Debate, Lakoff, G. Chelsea Green Publishing, 2014.

The Hidden History of American Democracy: Rediscovering Humanity's Ancient Way of Living, Hartmann, T. Berrett-Koehler Publishers, 2023.

The Hidden History of American Oligarchy: Reclaiming our Democracy from the Ruling Class, Hartmann, T. Berrett-Koehler Publishers, 2021.

Metaphors We Live By, Lakoff, G. & Johnson, M. University of Chicago Press, 1994.

On Tyranny: Twenty Lessons from the Twentieth Century, Snyder, T. Tim Duggan Books, 2017.

Red Brains, Blue Brains: Authoritarian We Will Go!, Robinson, S. Paleos Media, 2024.

Red Brains, Blue Brains: The Psychology of MAGA, Robinson, S. Paleos Media, 2024.

Star Trek and Humanism, Robinson, S. Paleos Media, 2023.

To Summon the Future, Robinson, S. Paleos Media, 2023.

ABOUT THE AUTHOR

Scott Robinson is an artificial intelligence designer, social scientist, public speaker and musician, and serves as Director of Technology and Content for the non-profit Humanity Prime. He has been published in *Rolling Stone* and *The Wall Street Journal*. He can be found at

scottrobinsonwriter@gmail.com